MY LIFE WITH MUSSOLINI

MY LIFE
WITH MUSSOLINI

by
RACHELE MUSSOLINI
in collaboration with
MICHAEL CHINIGO

London
ROBERT HALE LIMITED
63 Old Brompton Road S.W.7

© RACHELE MUSSOLINI 1959

First published in Great Britain 1959

PRINTED IN GREAT BRITAIN BY
EBENEZER BAYLIS AND SON, LIMITED, THE
TRINITY PRESS, WORCESTER, AND LONDON

CONTENTS

CONTENTS

LIST OF ILLUSTRATIONS

ACKNOWLEDGMENT

Illustrations Nos. 1, 2, 3, 4, 7, 8, 10, 11, 12 and 15
are reproduced from photographs supplied by
Radio Times Hulton Picture Library.

CHAPTER I

CHILDHOOD MISERY

Towards the close of the last century Predappio was a little hamlet like many others in Romagna. The ruins of an old castle gave it a dubious distinction, but the life of the community, as in other nearby boroughs, revolved around the only building of note: the Comune. It dominated a cluster of one-storey and two-storey stone and stucco houses whose ill-fitting, crude doors and windows and, above all, nondescript colour—the result of years of the dirt of poverty seeping into what was originally bright white plaster—bore witness to the struggle for life of the inhabitants. The hundreds of small vineyards which formed a framework to the little place provided a striking contrast: they were well-groomed and neatly kept. The "Romagnoli" lived first on the land and then in the home.

In this setting, and actually in the "sub-commune" of Predappio known as Salto, I was born in the early hours of 11th April, 1892, the fifth daughter and seventh child of Agostino Guidi and Anna Lombardi.

Time has tried to change Predappio, to make of it a small industrial centre. It has succeeded in part, but not enough to wipe away completely the eighteenth-century landscape. Behind the spotty veneer of progress still lies the sleepy little valley hamlet with many of the old buildings still intact.

One of these is the house where I first saw the light of day. It was an old house then. It had been occupied by my family for three generations, ever since my great-grandfather was employed by Count Ranieri Biscia, of one of Emilia's oldest aristocratic families, as factor on his estate. Subsequently the estate changed hands several times and was finally purchased by the Zoli family, who still own it today. They split it up into little farms for tenant-farmers. My family held on to the old house by bidding for and getting the plot of ground and vineyard surrounding it. We were tenant-farmers when I was born.

Salto had its main building, or "Palazzo" as we call it, too. It was a fifteenth-century structure. There were two "wells" in the cellars with remnants of various implements of torture. There were also two dimly-lighted chapels, one inside the

building, the other in the courtyard, which were still used for
religious services, and innumerable sinister-looking frescoes and
a legend of ghostly apparitions. My childish curiosity was set
ablaze. I made various sorties into this world of phantasy but
could never tour the whole palazzo. My thumping heart made
me an easy prey to imaginary voices, and noises, and I always
came out running—more frightened with each try. I finally
gave up, until later years—when I laughed at my childish
fears.

My two brothers died at an early age, and we five girls had
to take over the farm work as well as the running of the home.
At the tender age of four, I was in charge of the fowls and
driving the pigs and turkeys.

At the age of six I was responsible for a major crisis in our
household: I insisted upon going to school. To appreciate the
impact of my request on the family it should be remembered
that school was not obligatory in those days and only middle-
class children attended it. My sisters, who had not gone to
school themselves, regarded my request as a dodge to escape the
heavier farm work and their reaction was definitely hostile. But
my tears—and I shed many—finally won over my mother who
had the luck to learn how to read and write. She became my
great ally, and I finally went to school, even though it meant
walking twelve kilometres daily, and taking on my share of
work at home in the after-school hours to placate the resentment of my sisters.

At school the girls were accommodated on the second, and
the boys on the ground floor. I was a lively warm-hearted girl
and was speedily disillusioned when I found myself looked down
on by the other girls, who considered themselves city products
while I was only a country bumpkin. There was plenty of
stone-throwing between me and the scamps below. One day,
furious at an insult, I threw a big stone at a boy and hit him
on the cheek. The sight of blood frightened me. I ran home and
stayed there three days, until the teacher sent for me to return
to school. This incident seemed to persuade both boys and girls
to treat me if not with affection, at least with respect. And
strangely enough, the boy I struck became my best friend—a
friendship that lasted through the years until he died, a Blackshirt volunteer, in the Ethiopian campaign.

I had just finished my first-grade studies when our family was
evicted from the old Salto homestead. "Responsible" for the
eviction was, strangely enough, my eldest sister Giovanna,

whose marriage had unduly reduced the family's "labour force"—as the landlord put it. Shortly after Giovanna went to live with her husband ten kilometres away from Salto, he threw us out of the farm which three generations of our family had cultivated and developed to many times its original value. Giovanna's marriage was certainly a tremendous blow to the family fortunes, but it was a very happy union as far as she herself was concerned—she was blessed with fourteen children.

Father was pressed for time and managed to find a small house in Dovia—"a temporary arrangement," he called it. And it was this move that settled my destiny, for at the little Dovia schoolhouse I met the first member of the Mussolini family, Benito's mother, Rosa Maltoni Mussolini, my new teacher. I was immediately struck by her kind manner and goodness of heart and the deep sadness of her eyes seemed to pierce my very soul. Nor was I alone in my sentiments. She was loved by all the schoolchildren, who hung on her every word from the moment she entered the schoolroom from the house next door (where she lived with her family) to the moment she said the ritual "school is dismissed".

Alessandro, her husband, was the swarthy village blacksmith and the leading political figure as well. Between the thumps on the anvil his booming voice expounded socialist principles to the willing or more often unwilling ears of the customers. His temper and exuberance were responsible for frequent incidents which had unpleasant repercussions for his wife and three children, so much so that the number of students entrusted to Rosa's care dwindled with the years and in direct proportion to his "subversive" propaganda. The "signorotti" or landed gentry at one time asked for an investigation of the goings on at the school and forge, but the findings cleared the school-mistress. None the less, many of the children were kept by their parents from attending Signora Mussolini's school. She was very upset and poured her heart out to us, whom she called her "faithful flock". I have never forgotten her little speech—I've had cause to remember it again and again—which went something like this: "You know my trials and tribulations, but you can never understand what it means to work night and day to keep my children just above starvation—and to suffer the insults of those who don't know what it means to work."

Her eldest child, Benito, was then frequenting the *Scuola Normale* at Forlimpopoli, and during the vacation months he helped his mother by taking over some of the lessons in the little schoolhouse. He was only ten years older than I, but to me and the other school children he seemed an exceptional teacher who had an extraordinary gift for keeping us in order with his grave mien and firm voice. I seemed to be magnetized by his coal-black eyes.

Years later I learned that his attention had been caught by my long blonde pigtails and fidgety ways. The young master insisted on strict discipline and the methodical habits which marked his own work.

I was eight when my father died. The end came suddenly. He came home one night and hurried to bed, gently complaining that he was more tired than usual. Shortly before midnight his heavy breathing awakened mother, who shook him but got no reaction. Highly alarmed, she called my sister to the bedside and both stood helplessly by as poor father breathed his last without regaining consciousness. The town doctor, arriving some time later, told us that the cause of death was a heart attack.

It was 11th September, 1899—a day of tragedy for our little household. Father had barely been able to keep us clothed and fed. Now he was gone and with him the means and hopes for the morrow. He had left us completely penniless and we had no alternative but to ask the town to give father a pauper's burial—which cost twenty-four lire—and put us in the Poor Register. Dovia's town council first came to our aid with one kilogram of salt a month—salt cost twenty centimes per kilo—and even this little contribution was discontinued after three months. Our misery was beyond belief and, to make matters worse, Mother's health failed after Father's death. She seemed to have neither the wish nor the will to get well.

This was undoubtedly the most wretched period of my youth. The marriage of my second sister, Rosella, took place in this time of misery and squalor. I helped her with household duties and a year later, when her first child came, became both housemaid and nursemaid.

My schooling was thus interrupted. Moreover, I missed my mother and inadequate feeding and my sister's irritability (due to privations and overwork) were hard to bear. I put up with all this as long as I could, but ultimately my patience and endurance gave out and one morning I ran away without saying a word to anyone. As I walked the eleven kilometres to Dovia my heart pounded at the prospect of rejoining my mother and my mind was full of schemes for contributing to the household by working in the village. But my sister Augusta, who was alone when I arrived, gave me a very chilly reception. After telling me that Mother was away visiting her brother in the near-by town of Meldola, she rated me soundly for having "deserted" my other sister and said baldly that I had already given the family a lot of trouble.

Dangerous is the reaction of youth when embittered by sorrow and resentful of inexplicable harshness or mistreatment. I was no exception. My sister had dashed all my hopes, and given me a sense of revolt. I left the house at once to seek the hospitality of a kind woman neighbour who had befriended me in my infancy. She took me in, fed me and put me to bed.

The next day, to show the good lady my gratitude, I offered to take her two sheep to pasture and it was while I was playing the young shepherdess on the banks of the river Rabbi that Alessandro Mussolini, happening to pass that way, saw me, and talking to me like a father, urged me to spare my mother additional worries because her health was still poor. He personally informed her of my whereabouts and Mother came in person to fetch me home. She was very indignant with my sister.

It was now late autumn. My return and the coming winter, with the hardships it would bring with it, persuaded my mother to move to Forli, where we hoped to find work. Mother's brother was particularly anxious for us to go as he feared he would have us on his hands if we remained at Salto. To farmer folks like us the country seemed to offer a greater chance of a living while the city represented complete uncertainty. But in the circumstances, there was no alternative.

After selling a few pieces of the furniture, which constituted our only wealth, to cover the expense of moving the remainder, we moved to two tiny, dingy rooms in a back street in Forli. But what a blessing they were! And an even greater blessing was the fact that we all got employment. "Lean Luisa"—such was the nickname of a woman who ran an employment agency —found me a job as housemaid with a market gardener, and Mother and Augusta similar jobs in two different well-to-do families.

From the utter destitution at Dovia, we had moved upward one rung in Forli: we were now house-servants, all of us. A third sister, Pina, lived with relations at Carpena.

CHAPTER II

LOVE COMES ON SUNDAY

THE MARKET gardener, though poor himself, was forced to hire one girl-helper in order to cultivate his bit of ground. He offered me a salary of three lire a month and showed me my sleeping quarters—a little windowless cupboard under the stairs. I had no choice but to accept, because the need at home was really great. But the very first night was unbearable. I threw myself on the cot fully dressed, and cried all night without closing an eye. The next day I found out that the girl who had had the place before me had been taken to the hospital as a tuberculosis suspect. Greatly worried, I took my troubles to "Lean Luisa" who came to the rescue and next morning I was found a new job.

This time I was to be housemaid in the family of an N.C.O. in the artillery who was also a fencing instructor. I was delighted, because I had a nice little room in which I slept with my employer's small daughter. But complications soon arose to make my prospect of a steady job doubtful. Many officers, and civilians too, came for fencing lessons; the wife was still young and very pretty, while her husband was around fifty. Her behaviour was somewhat flighty. But I was too young to understand. I used to get up at five o'clock in the morning with the help of an alarm clock to get breakfast for my employer, who went to the barracks very early. Fear of losing my job made me careful to be very punctual and work very hard, but one day I broke a dish and my mistress wanted to dock me of two months' wages. Her husband came to my rescue, and afterwards treated me so kindly that I became very fond of him. In the early part of summer he had to go to Predappio for gunnery exercises, and before leaving, took me aside and said something to this effect: "Keep an eye on all visitors here during my absence, and if you see anything wrong, write me at once."

I kept my eyes open and noticed many things that had escaped me before. I was utterly disgusted. When I thought of the good and trusting man who was being betrayed I decided to leave the house at once. To save face, I left him a note that I was returning to Predappio to stay with my sister and thanking him for the kindness he had always shown me.

In Predappio I was fortunate enough to find immediate employment at Casa Lunga farm with a peasant family, the Frignani. Here I felt at home because they treated me as one of themselves and then there was the sunshine and healthy air of my home ground which more than compensated for the very hard work. Unfortunately, there was a stumbling-block in this family, too. The old master, nicknamed "Minaia", was jealous and very stingy, a real tyrant in his own household, following the rigid customs of the Romagna, where family life was fashioned on a medieval pattern. An "original" if there ever was one, he had a violent aversion to progress, which he considered a danger to the world. He used to call a train—something he had never seen at close quarters—an infernal machine, and would never travel by rail. To me he became a holy terror but even his own family feared him, because he ruled over everyone and everything with an iron hand and used to seal up the cupboards for fear someone would steal a piece of bread. One summer evening, after threshing, his daughter-in-law, who was pregnant, and I were cleaning up the house when "Minaia" rushed in and ordered us to go and mow the grass in the meadow. We were so tired that she refused. The old man in a furious rage, gave her such a beating that she had an abortion a few days later. But I put up with this and other scenes for two years before I finally made up my mind to return to Forli, where I entered service in the Chiedini family.

They were well off, the house was large and the pay excellent—eight lire a month. I worked with a will because the mistress treated me almost as though I were her own child. She was a lady of high moral and domestic virtues and from her I learned many things that were useful to me later in life. She was fond of saying, "You must learn to do everything; you might even become queen, but no one can ever say what the future has in store for you."

In 1908 I had some news of Benito Mussolini, the son of my last teacher, from Signor Chiedini who, having large landholdings, naturally opposed socialism. From him I learned that Mussolini had led a group of demonstrators who had seized some threshing machines in the sub-prefecture of Sansonino.

My master said, "Do you know they've arrested that crazy fool Mussolini? With his hair-brained ideas he thought he'd get one up on us. Don't forget that it's the man with the capital who holds the knife by the handle. Good luck to him."

Like many working people in those days, I sympathized with

the ideas of Mussolini and other socialists of Romagna, so I could not take Signor Chiedini's jibe in silence and blurted out, "There's nothing dishonourable about going to gaol for an ideal. All who work have a right to fair wages, enough for them to live on."

This was but one of many occasions on which I found myself defending the actions of the imprisoned young socialist agitator in the Chiedini household, and even in Forli itself. But Mussolini's confinement was short. At the trial a better advocate than the defending lawyer, Bonavita, was the accused himself, and it was his warm, impassioned appeal in a courtroom filled with friends and sympathizers that won him his liberty.

Hitherto, we had had nothing but vague reports of Mussolini's activities. After graduating as a school teacher at Forlimpopoli, he had taught in the elementary schools of Gualtieri Emilia, but after a short time, driven by desire for adventure and bigger earnings, had emigrated to Switzerland in hope of bettering his fortunes. In 1903 he was expelled from the Swiss Confederation and on his return to Italy enlisted in the 10th Berslaglieri, stationed at Verona. It was during this period, in February 1905, that, to everyone's sorrow, his mother, the schoolmistress Rosa Maltoni Mussolini, died. Upon his discharge from the army in the autumn of 1906, Mussolini again took up teaching in the elementary schools in Caneva di Tolmezzo. Then he went to France and afterwards taught in a college at Oneglia. It was on his return to the Romagna that he was arrested for his part in the affair of the threshing-machines.

I recall clearly—as if it were today—that Sunday morning in the autumn of 1908 which sealed my life's destiny.

I had just come out of church with Chiedini's little daughter. As was the custom then—and still is—we had lingered in the little square in front of the church to chat to friends and enjoy the sun. I heard my name called, turned around and found two coal-black eyes looking into mine. For a moment I saw nothing else—my heart was in my mouth. It was Benito Mussolini, but he was greatly changed from the days when he used to help his mother in the little Dovia schoolhouse. He had a small black beard—which did not prevent me from recognizing him immediately—and I noticed that his suit was threadbare in many places. His pockets were bulging with newspapers and he had some books in his hands.

His first words, "Do you still recognize me? I am Benito,"

struck my ears, already red with excitement, like hammer-blows.

His second remark, "But how you've grown up! You're quite a young lady!" uttered as he took me in from head to foot with a smile of curiosity, completed my bewilderment. I could not speak a word but he rescued me from my embarrassment by continuing in a most encouraging tone, "While I was away I often thought of the little girl who was always up to tricks in school at Predappio. Why haven't you come to see us?"

"I should like to have come, but my work prevents me and if Signor Chiedini came to hear of it, I'd certainly get it hot!"

He shook his head and, with eyes full of understanding, said, "Oh! These bosses! These bosses! They never let those who work for them have a moment to themselves. I know what work means; I've worked in one country after another from morning to night for a few lire. It's the lot of the poor." A simple wave of the hand in farewell, and he was gone.

Some time previously the Mussolini family had left Predappio for Forli where Benito's father, Alessandro, had opened a little inn near the railway station. My own mother had soon afterwards gone to live with him.

When I returned home from my meeting with Benito, I told Signora Virginia, my kind mistress, everything and begged her to let me visit the Mussolinis and my mother. She consented and I went the same day after lunch. It was a happy reunion. For a few hours we talked and laughed about one thing and another and I was glad to hear that business in the little inn was good, especially because Alessandro sold the wine he made from his own vineyards. We recalled people and events of old times in Predappio and I told them the full story of my strenuous and painful girlhood. But my past sufferings seemed to vanish in the presence of Mother, Benito and the others. Came the hour of parting and Benito insisted on taking me home. We walked side by side for a while without saying a word. Then he gave me details of his own struggle for existence and of how he had been a jack-of-all-trades—bricklayer's mate, school teacher, storekeeper, newspaperman. He also told me of his success as agitator and comrade of political agitators in exile. Of the numerous stories I recall this one best:

"I was walking one night with a chance acquaintance. I had joined him because I felt terribly alone. He was a strange type of Russian. He knew many languages and had many diplomas but was completely penniless. He was unemployed like me and had a sinister appearance. As we walked along I heard the ticking of an alarm clock and then noticed that it was tied around his wrist with a thick cord. I was amazed and asked, 'Have you stolen it?' He was hurt by my question and indignantly replied, 'Yes, sooner or later you too will have to steal.' At my retort that it would never happen he laughed bitterly and we parted.

"Two days later I was arrested by police for vagrancy and thrown into gaol. It was dark and it was only after several minutes that I began to notice the other occupants. Then one of them came towards me and said, 'So here you are yourself!' It was the owner of the alarm clock. I tried in vain to explain to him 'the crime' of which I was guilty. But his logic would admit no other alternative. Next morning I was freed but the Russian remained in gaol. As I was about to leave he cried out, 'As always, the clumsy beginners are the luckiest.' "

We laughed at what seemed funny at the time. Silence again and then Mussolini suddenly asked, "Why do you stay on with the Chiedinis? Come and live with us and be with your mother."

I made no reply. "I'm leaving Forli next week," he added. "I can't stand this town because it offers no possibility of the sort of work I want. I don't intend to go on being a schoolmaster; I'm just not cut out for it. I have something much bigger and finer in mind."

He confided to me that he had been invited by Cesare Battisti to work on the newspaper *Il Popolo* and even showed me a letter which had just come from Trento. Then he again repeated the invitation, "Come and stay with my family; I'm sure you'll be happier there."

"I'll think about it," was all my reply.

We reached the Piazza del Duomo and he invited me to have a cup of coffee with him, but I declined. In those days a girl's reputation, in Romagna at least, was seriously compromised if she was even seen in the company of a young man. Benito understood and we parted with a single handshake.

I spent a sleepless night. I was so happy at the prospect of ceasing to live with strangers and enjoying the warmth and affection of a family home. Life suddenly seemed easy and good.

When Signor Chiedini heard of my visit to the Mussolinis he was very angry and thereby gave me an excuse to leave his house at once and move to the Mussolini inn.

A few days later, as he had told me, Benito went away. On the eve of his departure we organized a little farewell party, a modest supper and a dance which lasted to the small hours of the morning. Benito seemed very happy and even played the violin. I noticed that he played well and was duly impressed. As the party drew to a close Mussolini took me aside and, fixing his extraordinary eyes on me said straight out of the blue, "I'm leaving tomorrow, but on my return you will become my wife. You must wait for me."

It was like a thunderclap. I managed a feeble laugh because I took it as a joke, and jokingly replied, "But supposing you don't come back?"

"I'll come back all right," he answered, and I had no doubt about his seriousness.

CHAPTER III

BIRTH OF EDDA

DURING his stay in Trento Mussolini sent only one post-card, and not to me but to his father. But it did include a P.S. for me, a reminder of what he had said before he left. It was quite natural that I should follow his doings in the eighteen months he stayed there. I knew that he was working with Cesare Battista and that his activities were regarded with suspicion by both the Austrian Government and the ecclesiastical authorities.

His period of residence was suddenly ended because, in a moment of irredentist fervour, he had written, "Italy does not end at Ala." The authorities ordered Benito's expulsion. A general strike was called in and around Trento as a protest against the action of the imperial police in arresting him and lodging him in Rovereto gaol. The strike threat induced the government not to prosecute but the expulsion decree was not withdrawn. Mussolini returned to Italy as poor as he had left it, with nothing but a little portmanteau and his inseparable violin. His father had to send him the train fare from the Austrian border to Forli.

I found him much improved in appearance. He was not so thin, had shaved off his beard and his clothes were less shabby, in fact, almost smart. He was obviously happy to see me again.

He smiled, which was unusual for him, and said, "I'm back, you see."

He told me a lot about his political and journalistic activities in Trento. Later on, when we knew each other better, he even dropped hints about his love affairs. But when he noted my evident embarrassment and disappointment he apologized and repeated his firm resolve to marry me, adding he would broach the subject to my mother and his father as soon as possible.

He had been back but a few days when the police were on his heels again. He was arrested, this time because of a fine imposed in a previous political trial which he had never paid. He was given an eighteen-day gaol sentence. His father, having had similar experience, attached little importance to the incident, but I dissolved into tears when a friend of Benito's, a certain Ferretti, communal secretary of Predappio, asked me to take him some food and books in gaol. I brought him food each day, and books I managed to get through his lawyer, Bonavita. Benito was very grateful. He served his sentence in a small cell in the Torrione della Rocca di Caterina Sforza and then resumed his contacts with his socialist friends in Forli with whom he decided to found a weekly newspaper. After wildly enthusiastic preparations the first number of the *Lotta di Classe*[1] appeared a few days later. The violence of his literary style was extraordinary. His articles had an aggressive thrust that at times frightened even his closest friends and the most rabid extremists.

Meanwhile, a young Ravenna surveyor, Olivieri, had asked me to marry him. He was of a well-to-do family and Benito's father, with his practical mind, favoured the young man's suit and even made the "matrimonial contacts" with Olivieri's parents. But I just could not bring myself to make up my mind what reply to give. Destiny already held me in its grip. When Benito heard about it he bitterly reproached his father and remarked curtly, "Rachele is to be my wife." Old Alessandro countered with fatherly advice, "Leave the girl alone. You've no job and no money. All you've got is your politics which will bring suffering to you and the woman who shares your life. Think of what your own mother went through because of me. You know what it means to keep and bring up a family. Rachele is a good girl and Olivieri can assure her a future of comfort and security."

They were sound arguments but not to Benito. There was no

[1] The Class War (tr.).

convincing him and he wrote in person to his rival, ordering him to leave me alone.

By now I was in love with him. I liked his fearlessness in facing and overcoming obstacles. I began to attend, sometimes in happy mood but generally with some apprehension, the public meetings at which he flung out his phrases like a challenge. It amazed me how he held the attention of his audience. But what I liked most was the kindness behind his apparent gruffness and pride. Yet the prospect of facing a life of storm and stress was quite discouraging because I could not forget all I had had to endure in my young life. So, though I loved him, I hesitated. But this did not daunt him; he knew he would win because he had always managed to get what he wanted. He was morbidly jealous. At one time he even forbade me to leave the house to go to work at the inn. He said he would rather work for me himself in any free time left him by his meetings and the newspaper. Then he forbade my attending his meetings, because, as he said, "When I see you I cannot speak."

One night he took me to the theatre. It was a completely new experience for me and I was thrilled and moved by the play, *La Cena delle Beffe*. When we came away at the end of the performance he said that the time had come to decide about our marriage. The consent of my family and his father would not be refused. "I want to create a life and a family. You must be my woman and the mother of my children."

It was a firm statement which precluded any reply. I said nothing. And he continued in gentler tones to speak of our future life as he dreamed it, of the children we would have—as though he would instil into me his exuberant vitality!

We parted. But the next day he summoned my mother and his father and, producing a revolver, gravely announced to them, in my presence, "There are six bullets, one for Rachele, the others for me." My mother, who knew the young man's resolute character, was the first to yield. Father Alessandro then followed suit, adjuring him to make me happy and adding a word of warning, "Your mother has suffered much from my politics. This girl cannot expect anything different with you."

Benito's decision precluded delays and one night, barely giving me time enough to get together my scanty wardrobe, he swept me off in a carriage to my sister Pina's house at San Martino, three kilometres from Forli. I was terrified, but completely dominated by his iron will. Nor was I without gloomy forebodings, but he swept them aside with his youthful confidence in the future, and I must admit that I was overjoyed to be so ardently desired.

I stayed with my sister while Benito looked for lodgings in the town at a rent possible to our straitened finances. He used to bring me copies of his *Lotta di Classe* fresh from the printer and point proudly to his contributions. I shared his views and always encouraged him. From the very outset I realized that nothing could deflect Benito from the path along which he was being irresistibly borne and, all fear departed, was ready to share his life so that after his hard day's labours he could have the consolation of an affectionate smile. I felt quite maternal towards him though I was ten years his junior—that tender feeling which is the secret of a woman in love. And he loved me for it.

Ultimately Benito found two furnished rooms in the palazzo Merenda, on the street of the same name, and we moved in one night. I remember how tired and happy he was, perhaps a little uncertain of my reaction—because the marriage papers were not yet ready. But I understood. I saw the man of my heart there before me, eagerly awaiting the only gift life could give him—my love—his young face already lined by his daily struggle. There was no hesitation. I went with him.

The two furnished rooms were small, but there was the advantage that the rent was low—only fifteen lire monthly—which we could meet with our budget of one hundred lire a month. Benito's salary at the Party weekly was one hundred and twenty lire a month but twenty went to Party funds. Our household belongings were limited to four bed-sheets, four dishes and a set of six knives, forks and spoons given to us by our parents. But we were immensely rich in youth and hope. I shall never forget the tranquil joy of that start together. Benito himself—later on—used to say that those first days had been the happiest of our lives. He was immersed in his work and I sang my Romagna folk-songs as I went about the daily chores of our little home, while outside the local political struggle raged ever more fiercely. The divisions between the parties were deep, and almost every night the wilder elements came to blows. The Socialists were opposed by the Republicans and both of them by the Conservatives. The struggle for power was also reflected in ruthless press polemics. Among the local political figures I remember Ezio Maria Gray, who edited the radical Nationalist weekly *La Difesa*. The *Lotta di Classe* did much to make Mussolini's name known; the paper was widely read and Benito's

articles were much discussed. The Republicans were led by
Pietro Nenni and published the *Pensiero Romagnolo*.

Cesare Battisti from Trento sent telegrams of encouragement
and solidarity and frequent were the messages of support from
French and Swiss Socialists and *émigrés* in the United States.
As a matter of fact, Mussolini's articles were so well liked in
American Socialist circles that they planned a large party under
Benito's management. He gave the proposal serious consideration and we might have gone, had not a new factor directed our
destinies otherwise. I became pregnant. It was with keen disappointment that we abandoned the idea of going to America.

On the 1st September, 1910, our first child, Edda, was born.
Benito could not register her as my daughter because we were
not yet officially married. Hence the stupid insinuation that
Edda was Benito's child by the Socialist agitator Angelica
Balabanoff.

My husband was most excited by Edda's arrival, and as his
emotions were always translated into a violent urge for action,
he threw himself into the political struggle with redoubled
fervour. But our joy was embittered by a fresh onset of the
paralysis which had attacked Benito's father Alessandro shortly
after our marriage. Benito himself had chosen Edda's name,
feeling certain I would bear a girl. Even then he was always
positive about everything. He was as delighted as could be, and
I discovered her father's strong features in the baby face and
was much moved. Benito went himself to buy a cradle—it was a
wooden cradle costing fifteen lire—and brought it home on his
shoulders.

Twenty-four hours after her birth, which was without complications, I was up and resuming my domestic duties.

CHAPTER IV

FROM PRISON TO *AVANTI!*

About that time Cesare Battisti invited Mussolini to resume
collaboration on his newspaper and suggested that he should
write a love story for it. Benito was inclined to refuse and I
myself had to persuade him. Thus was born *Claudia Particella*,
or, as the book later became known through the world,

The Cardinal's Mistress. The instalments brought fifteen lire apiece, but though they took him only a quarter of an hour, Benito soon tired of the job and wanted to leave the story unfinished. Battisti pleaded with him to continue because he considered it "very original", and said that the serial had increased the circulation of the newspaper. I myself advised him to give the plot a fresh turn and Benito finally yielded and decided to finish the story.

This novel was just a relaxation, for his real energies were concentrated on his political articles, written to defend the rights of labour. Often enough he failed to notice that our home was practically without the barest necessities. Our dinner was very frugal. Meat rarely found its way into our diet in which vegetables were the mainstay. Supper consisted generally of cabbage or endives and never satisfied our young appetites.

With his extremist views, my husband put off Edda's baptism and I did not insist, because, like other Romagna wives, I considered the will of my man law and followed it without question. There was an incident at Edda's eventual christening. A Republican employee in the city hall spread the rumour that Mussolini himself had brought his little daughter to the church and Benito was so angry at this political stunt that he sought out the culprit, who was "persuaded" by a couple of hearty clouts to deny the story, the sole purpose of which was to sow dissension among the Socialists.

A little later the health of my father-in-law became worse and one night, after asking to hold baby Edda in his arms, Alessandro Mussolini died. The funeral was attended by representatives of all the Socialists in Romagna, a final tribute to their old comrade. The distribution of the estate was swift and simple; Alessandro left a farm at Vallona, in the commune of Predappio, which was sold for nine thousand lire. That sum was divided among the three children and Benito gave the whole of his share to me.

Towards the end of 1910 Italians began to talk of Tripolitania and a majority of both Republicans and Socialists came out against a colonial war. Almost every night Benito harangued a crowd. The recall of classes to military service had far-reaching repercussions in the local political scene and our own little household was not spared.

By then we had moved to the Piazza Settembre. One day Benito was presiding over a meeting of the Camera del Lavoro to protest against the expedition to Tripoli, when a mob began to demonstrate against the Government. My husband and others—Pietro Nenni among them—tried to calm them down. At the railway station there was a train full of soldiers leaving for the port of embarkation. The crowd swarmed over the platform, boarded the train and forced the soldiers to get out. The police proved powerless to intervene. The local Republican leader, Lolli, was arrested and Mussolini and Nenni were put under strict police surveillance.

But Benito felt that his arrest would soon follow, and realizing the awkward position in which he would leave me and Edda, asked his lawyer and friend, Nenni Di Santa Sofia, to lend him five hundred lire. He made an appointment with Nenni at the Café Mararoni to collect the money, but two policemen arrested him as it was changing hands. They not only refused to let him send it to me but actually confiscated the five hundred lire. He was only allowed to send me a brief note and ten lire. But I was prepared for such incidents and when I saw a police-man coming to the door with an envelope in his hand, I knew what had happened. The policeman casually remarked, "We have arrested Mussolini," and as I just stared at him clutching little Edda in my arms, he asked me point blank, "Why don't you cry?" to which I simply replied, "Grief is not mended with tears." I shut the door on him, but when he had gone my nerves gave way and the tears came hot and fast. I had only twelve lire in the world and foresaw days of cruel hardship. Our Socialist friends gave me lots of help and the poorest were the most generous. Monti, Medri, and Attilio Utile deserve special mention.

Nenni also was arrested the same day and gaoled with Mussolini in the Forli prison. The defence was again entrusted to the friendly lawyer, Bonavita, but the interrogation lasted a long time and the days of anxiety stretched into months. I con-tinued to receive a small monthly allowance from the Party and managed as best I could. Once a week I used to take Mussolini food and try to comfort and encourage him. On the other six days various Socialist families, notably the Medris, looked after him. The Republicans in gaol did not receive similar attention and Nenni, for example, often went without his dinner because his friends "forgot" to take it to him. On more than one occasion I took him food and clothes entrusted to me by his mother—particularly when his wife was in hospital.

I succeeded in persuading the authorities to let Benito get Italian, French and German books and it was during this period that he began to learn German. In this dark, damp gaol, Benito also managed to finish a translation from Italian into French of a textbook in pharmaceutical chemistry. I used to visit him nearly every day, and on these visits I often met Nenni's mother and wife. The latter had a daughter slightly older than mine. The old mother and I spent much time commiserating with one another.

After three months Nenni, Lolli and Mussolini were transferred to the San Giovanni in Monte prison, Bologna. This was a heavy blow; at Forli the prisoners were surrounded by friends and sympathizers, while at Bologna they not only found themselves among strangers but mixed with common criminals. I wanted to join him immediately but had to hear from him first and news was long in coming. At length his letter came telling me that he was well but that the gaol was unbearably cold. I called on Nenni's mother and we decided to visit Bologna together. We had hardly enough money for the railway fare. We were allowed to see the prisoners and talk to them in the visitors' room. Immediately Benito asked me about Edda and was full of apologies because he was being kept away from us so long. As I choked back my tears, he asked me on the point of leaving to write to him as often as I could.

After three months, which seemed an eternity, the trial finally started at Forli. I had been allowed only one further visit. On this second visit, Nenni's mother, who had to look after her sick daughter-in-law and her baby, asked me to take her son Pietro a parcel but to say nothing about their troubles. The famous Forli trial ended with a sentence of a year's imprisonment and the costs. I am not easily floored but it was a dreadful shock. It was hard to take. Benito was furious and immediately appealed. He was taken back to Bologna pending the fresh trial.

For some time I had no news from him or about him, but one morning in February, 1912, Benito arrived unexpectedly, surrounded by a group of jubilant friends. He had won his appeal. I was speechless and all I could do was to thrust little Edda into his arms. She too showed her joy in her own way. I was really happy again, even though I fully realized that I had gained no more than a truce. By then Benito was quite incapable of abandoning the political struggle and avoiding its perils. He immediately got in contact with his old supporters and resumed his opposition to the majority of the Socialist Party.

The first time he revealed his immense strength of character was at the Party congress at Reggio Emilia when he succeeded in forcing the expulsion of reformist elements like Bissolati, Bonomi, Cabrini and Podrecca. His victory brought him nomination as a member of the Party directorate and the editorship of *Avanti!*, in place of Claudio Treves. The Party offered Benito the thousand lire a month salary which Treves had been receiving, but my husband did not want to overload the paper's funds and reduced the figure to five hundred. Among his colleagues were Bacci of Ravenna, Scalarini the designer and the Russian agitator, Angelica Balabanoff, a woman with a lively mind. His Forli friends regretted Mussolini's departure for Milan, but the Republicans were pleased because they were getting rid of an adversary they feared.

We joined Benito as soon as he had found a small apartment for us in Via Castel Morrone 19. The rent was a thousand lire a year and to me seemed enormous though I liked the house for its modern conveniences. My husband wanted to take all his books. To meet the removal expenses we had to sell part of our furniture. All we kept was our bed, Edda's crib, a kitchen table and cooking utensils. My mother came with us.

Mussolini worked night and day and Treves had to admit, somewhat grudgingly that *Avanti!* had been given a new lease of life, attributable to its fighting spirits. The organs of the other parties tried to counter Mussolini's attacks but his handling of their arguments whipped up the interest of his readers. Time and again Benito would confide in me and ask my judgment on his intimate thoughts and projects for the future. The original circulation of 12,000 copies of *Avanti!* gradually rose to 30,000, 50,000 and finally 100,000 by Mussolini's efforts. And to this exceptional journalistic success, Benito added intensive political activity in the shape of innumerable conferences, speeches and Party gatherings. His aversion to Freemasonry became more and more pronounced and his name now became known even beyond the frontiers of Italy as he came into touch with personalities of International Socialism, many of whom he had already met when he lived in Switzerland. In the various Swiss cantons he had moved in circles where exiles were wont to gather and, among other Russians, he had met and known Lenin himself. He admired these exiles for all they had endured in support of their ideals and the personal disinterestedness which was his own dominant characteristic.

I recall that Benito used to write his editorials and articles at high speed. They never took him more than a quarter of an hour.

It was my task, of course, to furnish our home and I undertook to accomplish it a little at a time, starting with the bare necessities. Benito was in favour of buying on the instalment plan but I have always disliked this system. My belongings might be few and poor, but at any rate they would be my own from the start. He let me have my way. I did all the work——cleaning, ironing and cooking—myself and I used to walk a considerable distance to shop at Verzieri market to save a few pennies. And I always made a point of seeming perfectly happy when I was with my husband so as not to add to his worries.

We were fast approaching the eve of the First World War— an event which marked a new and decisive milestone in the story of Benito's life and mine.

CHAPTER V

FROM INTERVENTIONISM TO WAR

WHEN THE time comes to tell the whole story from the beginning and without partisan passion, the birth of Fascism will have to be attributed to Mussolini's decision to back Italy's entrance into the war against Austria. This decision was inspired by a desire to give Italy just and secure frontiers in the north-east, the Adriatic and the Alps. He arrived at it only after profound reflection, because the policy of the Italian Socialist Party, of which he had become the leading exponent, was based on neutrality, internationalism, anti-militarism and humanitarianism.

In the early years, Mussolini followed this party line, but soon the profound concern for national interests which had always existed deep down in the Romagna Socialists and the Dovia blacksmith, was not to be denied. The persuasive tongues of several left-wing interventionists such as Fillipe Corridoni, Massimo Rocca (Libero Tancredi), and others also had their effect. The first open break between Benito and his party comrades came at a meeting of the party directorate at Bologna and brought his resignation from *Avanti!* He even refused the compensation which was offered to him as of right.

When he returned home from the meeting he told me of the split and quickly added, "Rachele, we're back to the hard times at Forli. I have no paper and no money. Edda is still a tot and life's going to be tough. But come what may I've decided: interventionist to the end."

Soon after, in an effort to find a job, he went to Genoa where his friend Captain Giulietti lent him two thousand lire. During his absence I had a surprising and unpleasant experience. A woman whom I did not know, much older than I, thin and apparently in a great state of excitement, knocked on the door, demanded to see Benito, entered without being invited, made a tour of the house and asked Edda if her father loved me. I calmed her down and eventually got rid of her. On his return Benito explained to me that he had had a brief affair with her (it was quite consistent with his impulsive nature) and that she was a nurse of Austrian origin, now living in Milan. Her name was Ida Dalser, and she was certainly mad, so much so that she once even set fire to the furniture in an hotel room, saying she was Mussolini's wife and that he would pay for the damage. I mention the incident because the police to whom the hotel owner had denounced the woman came and arrested me and I was kept in gaol for forty-eight hours until the misunderstanding was cleared up. It has been said that an illegitimate son resulted from this casual liaison and that he died in his teens.

Benito was noisily expelled from the Socialist Party at a meeting of the Milan comrades called for the express purpose. He proudly defended himself, concluding his speech with the words, "You hate me today because you still love me." Not all his former friends abandoned him. Some followed him, and were faithful to the end and shared his fate. One whom I particularly remember was Sandro Giuliani, who later succeeded Michele Bianchi as managing editor of the *Popolo d'Italia*.

Months of forced inactivity followed for Benito and it meant hard times for the family during which I had to perform real miracles in the way of economies. More than once I skipped my own meals to give Benito, Edda and my mother enough to eat. I did it without a thought because I felt it my duty to alleviate my husband's sufferings and worries in that difficult period. Of course he had had to drop the political review *Utopia* which he had begun to publish just before he severed his connection with *Avanti!*

The hostility of the Socialists towards Mussolini increased from day to day and the columns of his old newspaper were used by his former colleagues to shoot poisonous articles and satirical caricatures at him. I even noticed that some of the "comrades"—men like Giovanni Bacci of Ravenna—used to come to our home to profess their attachment to the old editor-in-chief and then return to the newspaper and publish vitriolic attacks on him. It was behaviour like this which amazed and hurt Mussolini most, because it was so wholly out of keeping with his way of life. Striding up and down the room, he would say, as much to himself as to me: "I *must* have a paper of my own; I can't write for other papers because it would seem like begging."

Thus was born the idea of the *Popolo d'Italia*. It quickly took shape in many lively discussions which went on for hours in our house between him and a few friends, who were rich only in initiative and ideals. I well remember Giuliani, Nicola Bonservizi, Lido Caiani, Gino Rocca, Giacomo di Belsita and Manlio Morgagni, who went from pillar to post in an effort to raise funds. At the start their hopes had the concrete backing of a few lire, which were entrusted to me for safe keeping and guarded as jealously as if they were the state treasury. More money was collected by subscription and advances on advertising. I remember a spontaneous donation of two thousand lire from Leonida Bissolati.

A few rooms were found in Via Paolo da Cannobio 35, small, dark and without furniture. In the hole-in-the-wall which was to be the editor's office there was only a moth-eaten desk, one chair, and a few wooden boxes. These were the offices. Finding a plant willing to print the paper long proved an insurmountable obstacle. As for the title, it was chosen because Mussolini used to say that he intended to work "for all the Italian people, from the Alps to the sea". To the mast he nailed Blanqui's words, "He who has steel has bread." I asked Benito if he really believed it and got the resolute answer, "The most essential thing for the life of a nation is the army and governments must never forget it. He who is strong also has enough to eat because he can always get it."

In those days an individual of foreign nationality, but living in Italy, paid a visit to our home and was brave enough to suggest to my husband that he should run his newspaper for the benefit of Austria. In exchange Benito would be given anything he asked. I was in the next room and heard my husband's angry reaction; I went to the door in time to hear him shout out, "Get out! Millions can't buy ideals. Rachele, show this man the door."

The visitor was taken aback for a moment; then he clasped Mussolini's hand and said, "I admire you."

The first issue of the *Popolo d'Italia* came out on 15th November, 1914, and was an immediate success, despite the sabotage tactics of its enemies. They even persecuted the retailers and newsboys, but circulation increased rapidly, and in the space of a few months reached the hundred thousand figure to which Mussolini had previously raised *Avanti!*—whereas the Socialist Party daily lost ground. Our enemies sarcastically dubbed Benito's dingy offices "The Lair", but Mussolini liked it, and it stuck.

My husband and I used to test the public's reaction to *Popolo d'Italia* by visiting the kiosks and street vendors incognito. The answer in Milanese dialect was always the same, "They all like it, particularly when that man Mussolini writes. If I knew him I'd tell him to write an article every day."

One evening in January 1915, Benito came home with two men whom he introduced as Fillipe Corridoni and the Marquis Paolucci di Calboli. He explained that as the result of their advocacy of intervention they had been forced to leave Parma and Forli respectively. They had met in the Piazza del Duomo during one of Mussolini's public meetings. Paolucci sadly remarked, "Romagna is a difficult country, the Romagnoli are intelligent but at times they won't use their brains. This war is necessary and we shall enter it." From that day these two men stood by my husband, and at more than one disorderly meeting he owed his personal safety to their intervention. The police sometimes dispersed the demonstrators with their batons and Benito, who couldn't keep out of a fight, came home time and again with his clothes half torn off and his hat battered.

Then came the declaration of war. "The goal of my paper has been reached," Mussolini told me that night, "but there's still lots to be said and done to back up the men in the firing line."

The war indeed proved to be a tough business, as we were short of munitions and the battleground was most difficult. Benito volunteered at once and asked to be sent to the front, but the authorities replied that they could not accept him because the call-up of his class was imminent. The summons came in a matter of days. He joined the 11th Bersaglieri and after a short time at Verona was sent to Ferrara. I joined him there for a few days, which were very happy. Then, in September 1915, he left for the front. I did not see him for several months and could only follow his military career in the letters he wrote me every day and the articles he sent to the *Popolo d'Italia*.

His departure brought us a new period of privation. The newspaper was ours, but the monthly payment of five hundred lire was never paid on time by the business manager, Morgagni, either because he was slack or perhaps was too involved in difficulties of his own. We also suffered from the early bombardments. I well remember the very first one, which was quite unexpected. It was Sunday morning when three aeroplanes arrived, flying low. At first no one paid much attention; then the first bombs began to explode, starting a great panic in the city. Some ten dead and one hundred wounded. I had a big shock and since then have always hated air-raids.

Benito's letters kept me informed about the fighting and the morale of the troops. I also knew that the food was scanty and poor. On Christmas Day, 1915, my husband wrote, "The ration today was five desiccated chestnuts, but the lads are keeping their chins up." Suddenly I had news that Benito was down with paratyphoid. I set off at once for the hospital at Cividale, where he had been taken. I travelled in a cattle truck full of mules. When I arrived he was in a high fever, but already out of danger. During my brief visit he once remarked, "What do they say in the cities about all the *embusqués*? I suppose that we fighters will be looking round for a bit of bread when we return while that lot will be claiming they have won the battles. The men are furious." He himself was particularly upset by the wide-spread defeatism on the home front which blocked the path to victory. I returned from the hospital in a melancholy and anxious mood. The situation in Milan had deteriorated, especially on the food front. On one occasion there was no bread for five consecutive days—but no lack of dancing and other amusements.

Benito and I continued our indefatigable correspondence and I was soon able to tell him I was again pregnant. On 27th December, 1916, I wired him the birth of our second child, our son Vittorio. Benito chose the name in anticipation of the victorious end of the war. I was sorry that he could not see the child immediately, but I knew he had been transferred to a very dangerous sector on the Carso, a rocky valley where he was in fact to remain for six months.

Late one night in January 1917 I heard someone pounding at the door, "Open, Rachele. It's Benito." His voice was tired and I hardly recognized the ragged, battered soldier, with

Rachele Mussolini

The house in Predappio near Forli where Benito Mussolini was born

Benito Mussolini visiting the village school at Forlimpopoli where many years before his mother had been school mistress and his future wife a pupil

barbed wire doing duty for buttons. After refusing leave many times, he had decided to accept it. He spent most of his time in the *Popolo d'Italia* offices and even in the few days available contributed a fresh impulse. As he was leaving he said, "I'm afraid I won't get back in one piece next time, and his tone was so grave that I was greatly worried.

I remembered that remark a few months later when I was notified by telegram that Benito had been seriously wounded.

CHAPTER VI

FASCISM

Manlio Morgagni, our friend and the business manager of *Popolo*, was the first to see Benito in the military hospital in Rochi and the first to give me the details of how he had been wounded: he had been serving with a mortar battery and the barrel of one of the mortars had become overheated. He drew his officer's attention to the fact but the latter ordered him to carry on loading, whereupon the weapon exploded. Five of the crew were killed instantly and several wounded—among them Benito, who was taken half naked to the nearest dressing station and then to hospital. He had a number of wounds of which the worst was in the left thigh. A bomb fragment had shattered the bone and carried dirty pieces of cloth into the wound. The military surgeons despaired of his life but his tough fibre triumphed. To make matters worse, the Austrians began to bombard the hospital and though the patients were transferred to dug-outs, his condition was too serious for him to be moved. After a consultation, it was decided to amputate Benito's left leg. In his delirium Mussolini kept saying, "Do what you like." At the last minute someone suggested a less serious operation as the result of which the leg was ultimately saved.

Life at the hospital was monotonous. From time to time he wrote me that various friends had been to see him and in one of his letters he described visits from King Victor Emmanuel and some British and French generals. When his condition permitted he was transferred, first to Udine and then to Milan. There I found him unrecognizable. The only thing left was the old flame in his dark eyes—a rather sad little flame in the deathly pallor of his face.

3

It was our second meeting in a hospital. His first words were, "I really thought I'd never see you again, but now I'm with you I feel I'll pull through." We decided that I must stay at the hospital and Dr. Ambrogio Binda, Benito's close friend, who was looking after him, authorised me to wear Red Cross uniform and work as a nurse, hiding my identity. Every three or four days his wounds had to be dressed, and he suffered great pain. The disguise worked for some months but one day the Director of the hospital, a dentist from Parma who later committed suicide when his illicit gains through speculation were discovered, saw through it all and forced me to leave. My worries had reduced me to a shadow; I weighed under seven stone, so Benito suggested that I should go to Luino to get some country air and build myself up. I took Vittorio with me while Edda stayed behind and was to bring Benito to join us as soon as he was allowed to leave the hospital. He was particularly fond of Edda whom he called the "child of sorrow" because she was born to us at our worst moment.

When the Italian forces were routed at Caporetto, Mussolini, whose left hand was still semi-paralysed by a bomb splinter, wrote a series of rousing articles from hospital which kept alive the spirit of resistance and largely contributed to that revival which eventually brought us victory.

When he left hospital Benito resumed his duties as editor of *Popolo d'Italia*, though still in pain and using crutches. For over two years, day in day out, I used to meet him every night at the main door of our block and help him to negotiate the stairs to the fourth floor where we lived. There was no lift.

The war ended a year later with victory for Italy and our little family had visions of a quiet, comfortable home life. We were quite pleased with our little house. Edda already played the violin well—she had begun at the age of four, when the ten lire per lesson charged by her teacher bit deep into our resources. But I paid it gladly because Benito, even while at the front, had urged me to have Edda taught music. It was a real joy to all of us to see the little tot so keen on playing the violin. Normally, her features were a soft replica of Benito's, but when she played the firmness of the jaw, the protruding cheek-bones, the pursed lips, the penetrating look, produced an even greater resemblance to her father. From the very start, Edda displayed a surprising feeling for music and Benito was proud that his daughter possessed the same artistic temperament as his own.

Edda was extremely jealous of her brother Vittorio and when
he was born she had fits of depression because she feared that
our affections would now be stolen by the new baby. She could
even be spiteful. One day she even pulled the chair from under
her grandmother while she held Vittorio in her arms. Vittorio,
on the other hand, was not saddled with the morbid sensitivity
of his sister and greeted the birth of our third child, Bruno, with
enthusiasm. I understood the temperaments of my children and
loved them equally.

I cannot recall Bruno's birth without associating it with a
humorous anecdote. Benito had not been present at the birth of
Vittorio—he was at the front—and was quite annoyed about it.
He used to say, "I always have to hear the best news about my
own family from strangers." When the happy event was still a
month ahead Mussolini was already cutting down his meetings
and journeys so that he might be present when it happened.
But one day he had to go to Genoa. It was urgent business and
we were still some time away from the scheduled visit of the
stork. There was no need to worry. Before leaving he nevertheless impressed on me the importance of waiting for him and
promised to rush back as soon as possible. He had hardly left
Milan, however, when the first pains came and the child was
born so quickly that the midwife I had summoned did not
arrive in time to assist me. Benito arrived the following evening
very angry. Morgagni had told him of the new arrival when he
met him at the railway station. There was a scene, and I always
remembered his remark, "But couldn't you wait for me?" Then
he was the first to laugh.

Then came the period of mob agitation, chain strikes and
hostility to the war veterans. Mussolini lost no time in cham-
pioning the cause of the veterans and made the *Popolo d'Italia*
their mouthpiece. The newspaper's offices became like a port of
call for all who refused to repudiate the victory. So far as
possible, assistance was never refused to the unemployed. The
stream of men asking for help became so great that when a
visitor was announced, Benito, without raising his head from
his work, would say, "Give him ten lire." It had become
routine.

I certainly do not propose to relate the political history of
that time or the years following. It is too well known and any-
how I do not consider it my business. I am concerned solely to
record my memories of my husband in the years we lived
together. But I cannot let the date of the foundation of the

"Fasci"[1]—23rd March, 1919—pass unnoticed. "The programme," Mussolini told me, "will be primarily revolutionary-socialist but with sufficient patriotism and nationalism to exploit the victory of which we are being robbed by our former allies—as has happened at Versailles—and the defeatism of the extremists at home whose neutrality was frustrated in 1914."

Mussolini did not share the hopes that many Italians pinned on Woodrow Wilson. His suspicions were unfortunately only too strongly confirmed during Wilson's visit to Italy. At a reception given to the American President, Benito had the opportunity for a talk with him. He came home very agitated and remarked, "Wonderful welcome for the President, but he's far from bringing us the solutions we expected. His peace treaty gives us only the crumbs of victory. It will certainly sow the seeds of a new conflict."

The first "Fasci" were formed against this background. Progress was slow at first; then the movement gathered momentum and, starting with Reggio Emilia and Lombardy, the "Fasci" spread the length and breadth of the peninsula and the islands.

I well remember the men who were Mussolini's close collaborators in this historic period. Most of them had been with him since the foundation of *Popolo d'Italia* in 1914: Umberto Pasella, Nicola Bonservizi—great friend of baby Edda who used to bring her toffee every day; he was assassinated in Paris by Italian exiles a few years after—Michele Bianchi, Leandro Arpinati, Manlio Morgagni—who later became head of the Stefani News Agency, and shot himself when he heard of the Duce's arrest on 25th July, 1943—Sandro Giuliani, Mario Carli the futurist poet, F. T. Marinetti, Mario Gioda, Ferruccio Vecchi—who led the action squads in the first Fascist demonstrations, and later dedicated himself almost exclusively to sculpture.

The *Popolo* and the political organization of the "Fasci" now completely absorbed Benito's activity. It was intensified when the poet Gabriele d'Annunzio marched from Ronchi to Fiume "to defend", as he said to my husband, "the Italian character of this zone which is being threatened by Slav and allied plotting". I was with Benito the night of 11th September, 1919, when d'Annunzio told him of his plans. We had gone to the theatre—one of the few occasions my husband had tried to escape for a moment from his work and worries and I had been

[1] Fasci Italiani di Combattimento.

able to accompany him. At the end of the performance, as we
were about to leave, a letter was brought to him and he opened
and read it, first in silence and then out to me. It said : "Dear
friend. The die is cast. I am leaving at this moment. Tomorrow
I shall take Fiume by assault. May Italy's God be with us. I
have left a sick bed and am still feverish, but postponement is
impossible. Once again the spirit shall dominate the miserable
flesh. Summarize the article which the *Gazzetta del Popolo* will
publish but give the last part in full and back our cause whole-
heartedly during the conflict. I embrace you. Your Gabriele
d'Annunzio."

Mussolini decided to support the Fiume enterprise in every
way and used the *Popolo d'Italia* in a drive for subscriptions for
the "Legionaries" which met with a generous response. Three
million lire was raised. In another drive to procure clothing for
the poor of Fiume Milan outdistanced all other cities. The
Milanese also vied with each other in providing homes for
Fiume children sent for safety to Italy. We ourselves took in one,
Adelmo Monti, aged nine, whom we later sent to the Parma
Conservatory to study the violin, but of whom we have had no
news since.

It was during that exciting time that I fell victim to an attack
of the "Spanish" influenza which had assumed the proportions
of an epidemic in Italy. I was breast-feeding Bruno and worried
over the danger of infecting him. But my mother's devoted care
pulled me through in a matter of days.

Benito decided to visit d'Annunzio in Fiume and, evading
the rigid police surveillance, boarded a "SVA", taking off from
Novi Ligure near Genoa. After the meeting he made the return
flight the same way, but engine trouble necessitated a forced
landing at Aiello near Udine. The airport officials, who were
supposed to arrest him, were put in a very embarrassing position
but could not refrain from giving him a most cordial reception.
From the airport Mussolini proceeded almost immediately to
Florence where a national congress of the "Fasci de Combattimento" or Fascist Action Squads was waiting for him. On
his way back to Milan, the car in which he was travelling with
friends ran into a level crossing which had been closed though
there was no train in sight or even expected. Quite naturally
an attempt on his life was suspected. He was thrown some
thirty feet and landed on a gravel heap. Though he was much
bruised, there were no broken bones. Leandro Arpinati and
the chauffeur were seriously injured.

The national elections in November constituted the outstanding event that autumn. In the Fascist Party list figured, besides Mussolini, the names of many men prominent in Italian politics and the arts, notably the conductor Arturo Toscanini, the poet Marinetti, Podrecca, and Major Baseggio. They fought a valiant fight in Milan which was dominated by extremist left-wing masses. At Lodi there was actually a fight and the Fascists Arpinati, Bonaccorsi and Gravelli were arrested.

CHAPTER VII

CONFESSIONS OF AN ANARCHIST

On the night of the elections Benito telephoned me towards eleven o'clock to tell me that the defeat was complete and a raging mob were demonstrating in the Galleria against him and his colleagues on the Fascist list. "Don't be alarmed," he added, "if the crowd should come to the house. Think of the children and if I'm not back by tomorrow it will mean I'm either dead or in gaol." It was not of course the first time he had spoken like that. There had been plenty of previous occasions on which I had had to screw myself up to reply, "Don't worry; I'll put the babies somewhere safe." This time "somewhere safe" meant a windowless garret in our block.

I carried out my promise and then looked up and down the street. Then I waited. From the nearby Socialist headquarters a strange funeral procession escorting three coffins with the names of Mussolini, d'Annunzio and Marinetti scrawled on the sides was moving towards the house. It was a grotesque masquerade and the flickering light from flaming torches made it seem even more sinister in the inky darkness. The mob stopped under our windows and began to yell, "We've got Mussolini's corpse in here." I ran up to the attic and grabbed the hand-grenades my husband had once brought back from the front. But luckily the unwelcome visitors were content with beating on the main door and then clattered off.

Victory was celebrated all that night and next day in the most indecent fashion, while I waited for news of my husband. Eventually a policeman, who used to patrol our beat, came and had a word with our commissionaire: "I'm sorry for that poor girl; tell her her husband is in San Vittore prison but don't let her know I said so." His indiscretion raised my spirits a bit. Soon afterwards Benito was released. Truth requires me to say that he owed his liberation to the unsolicited intervention of Arturo Toscanini and the editor of the *Corriere della Sera*, Luigi Albertini, who certainly was not a political sympathiser. When my husband got home his return was celebrated not only by me but by his colleagues and followers. He was in a merry mood. "What a pity," he said, "just when I was letting up for a bit!"

Commenting on the election defeat, which had been complete as the Fascist list had obtained only four thousand votes, he resolutely remarked, "We'll just have to begin all over again."

A new misfortune this time, a domestic one, then descended on us: Bruno's serious attack of diphtheria. When the lives of his children were at stake, Mussolini suffered intensely. From the thrusting man-of-action whom so many feared and admired he became just a father, worrying, despairing, praying, like millions of ordinary fathers throughout the world. The crisis was tremendous. I held Bruno in my arms for twenty-four hours, bending low over him to listen to his faint breathing. At long last he improved, but not without a bronchial-pulmonary complication. He was reduced to skin and bones. When the period of convalescence began he weighed only fifteen pounds.

The election results, on the contrary, did not worry Benito too much. He threw himself with renewed vigour into the reorganization of the Fasci, employing the men who had remained faithful—a task which kept him busy night and day. His sole relaxation in those days of nervous tension were his first flying lessons which he took from the ace Redalli at the Bresso airport.

Disorders, kidnappings and murders continued to plague the national political scene. One of the worst tragedies occurred in Milan at the Diana Theatre, near Porta Venezia. During the performance of an operetta, a time bomb hidden backstage by anarchists exploded, killing a large number of the very select audience. The number of victims of all the political parties struggling for power mounted as the fight became more and more ruthless. I recall the death, for example, of twenty-two-year-old Aldo Sette, victim of an ambush. In his dying moments he asked to embrace Mussolini. His own mother came to beg my husband to satisfy this last wish. Benito arrived in time. When he got back he was overcome with emotion: "That boy makes me feel certain that all this blood had not been shed in vain!"

During the night of 1st March, 1921, I dreamed that a plane piloted by Benito had crashed in flames. I have often had tele-

pathic warning of coming events. The moment I woke I begged
my husband not to fly that day. He laughed at my presenti-
ments but appeared to yield to my entreaties, so much so that
he left his flying jacket at home. I was still very worried, however, and the premonition that something was about to happen
remained. Hours later I was called up on the telephone and an
unknown voice said, "I've accompanied the Director to the
hospital at Porta Venezia, but don't be alarmed." Then I
heard Mussolini himself calling out, "Give me that receiver; I
want to talk to my wife. Don't worry, Rachele," he said, "the
plane crashed alright, but there are no broken bones." He
laughed and hung up. After an anxious hour's waiting I heard
a carriage stop at the door. I ran downstairs and saw my husband hobbling out, helped by his friend Binda. His head was
hidden by bandages. I was so exasperated that I screamed at
him, "It serves you right," and then burst into tears. "Don't
upset yourself, Rachele, it's nothing. I've cracked my legs a bit,
but my head's tougher than steel."

Binda added a few details: "Five stitches in the head and the
left knee fractured" (the same leg that was injured during the
war). "The aircraft completely destroyed." Benito suffered a
great deal and one night his temperature rose to 104 degrees.
It became necessary to operate to remove a blood clot under
the knee cap. After surgical treatment he improved but was
kept in bed for three weeks.

Mussolini's convalescence was marked by a strange incident.
A young man called the porter of our block and asked about
Benito's daily habits—what time he left the house and when he
returned. The porter, a woman, who was very fond of us, was
unfavourably impressed by the stranger's behaviour and
dubious appearance and insisted upon knowing why he wanted
to know. "I just want a job," the young man replied and left.
Next day he returned and insisted on speaking to Mussolini or
me. While the porter was making up her mind, our three
children passed her lodge—they had been playing in the street
—and offered to bring him up to our apartment. I opened the
door myself and asked the visitor what he wanted. He seemed
surprised at the children kissing me and the ease with which he
had got in. I mistook his shyness for embarrassment at his own
poverty and encouraged him to talk, assuring him I would plead
his cause with my husband, though it was unnecessary because
he always did his best to help anyone appealing to him. He did
not thank me, which surprised me. I went to the bedroom to

talk to Benito about him. During my brief absence he asked the children how many rooms we had, how many servants, and what Mussolini generally ate. He was obviously surprised to hear there were no servants, and that I did the cleaning and cooking. On my return I found the children engaged in animated conversation with him. I told him that Benito would see him at the newspaper offices in a few days' time. Before long Mussolini was able to leave the house on crutches. Dr. Binda and I were with him and glad to see him on his feet again.

At the main door, I recognized the young stranger and pointed him out to Benito who told him to go to the office and he would be helped. We left in a car and the young man waved to us. He kept his right hand in his pocket and I could never have guessed what thoughts were passing through his head. When Benito came in that evening he said that the young man's visit had been singularly dramatic. He had thrown a revolver on the desk, saying that the bullets had been destined for Mussolini but he was glad to have discovered the truth before committing a crime. He went on to explain that he was an orphan from Piombino and, being hard up, had got in with a band of anarchists who wanted Benito murdered. They gave him an advance of ten thousand lire and promised him an additional twenty thousand when the job was done. They stuffed his young head with ideas about Mussolini being wealthy and living like a prince; in short a traitor to be removed. The attempt on Mussolini's life was to have been made at the Dal Verme Theatre during a Fascist rally but the assassin designate had been unable to carry out his assignment because Mussolini, as a result of the plane incident, had been too ill to attend. He was now asking for work and a chance to escape from the anarchists. Benito arranged to send him to Trieste, but the Milan police had learned of the plot and arrested him on the Trieste train. My husband's intervention procured his release and the would-be murderer became a life-long friend.

We were living now in Foro Bonaparte 18, to which we had moved from Via Castel Moroni during the last year of the war, Benito's brother Arnaldo joining us until he was able to find a flat for his wife and children who had fled from their home town ahead of the Austrian invasion. (In their race to safety they had been machine-gunned by Austrian planes and in the nine-day odyssey Arnaldo's wife's hair had turned completely white.)

It was at Foro Bonaparte that another strange incident

occurred in the winter of 1920–21. For several days we noticed
a man leaning against a tree near our house. His appearance
was not alarming despite his long beard and shabby clothes.
Apparently just another down-and-out. But the way in which
he stayed in the same place made us suspicious. When Benito
passed by the man would nod and walk away. One day, to
clear up the mystery, Benito ran after him and asked him the
reason for his odd behaviour. The man's story was a sad one.
He was a former army officer of good family but had been
reduced to begging, a thing he had never had the courage to do.
I saw Benito run into the house and search the cupboards for
clothes and underwear. "Give me some bread as well," he said.
He ran out without a word of explanation. From the window
I saw him give everything to the stranger. Some time went by
and the incident was forgotten. My husband's life was becoming
more and more hectic, with its ever increasing work and
interests and he had to take taxis from the office to his meetings.
One night he took a taxi off the rank as usual, but when he
offered to pay the driver at the end of the journey the money
was refused. "Don't you recognize me?" said the driver. "I'm
the stranger whose life you saved last winter; you also saved my
family by finding me this job. You must let me give you at
least one free ride; I can't pay you back any other way."

I mention the incident of the ex-army officer whom my
husband befriended, not for the story itself, but because his case
was typical and his troubles were those of thousands of Italian
officers and soldiers who were trying to return to civilian jobs
in the face of organized opposition and left-wing propaganda
directed at discrediting all who had fought in the war.

CHAPTER VIII

OCTOBER 1922

THE 1921 election was to be the acid test. It was to show
whether Mussolini's effort to rebuild the Party organization
from the ground up after the 1919 fiasco had borne fruit.
Excitement ran high when the first results began to come in.
Mussolini was confident from the start and many of his friends
were quietly hopeful. But complete returns spelled an im-

pressive victory. The Fascists, forming a *bloc* with various parties, including the World War 1 veterans, had elected an appreciable number of deputies to the Italian Chamber.

There was celebration of course, though on a modest scale. At its climax, the radiant Benito exclaimed, "Rachele, we are about to live the finest days of our lives." That first election success brought the Fascist Party a new wave of sympathisers and a rush for membership which multiplied Mussolini's duties and responsibilities. In the Chamber of Deputies Benito's speeches were few but to the point, and they were listened to in almost religious silence. But he preferred to wage his battle for power primarily from the columns of the *Popolo d'Italia.*

There were many quarrels, which were often settled by duels —more than ten of them. There was one with Colonel Baseggio, others with the Socialist Ciccotti and the anarchist lawyer Merlin and so on. Mussolini never referred to these duels at home. But soon I got wise to a tell-tale trick to which Benito resorted. He used to eat spaghetti after each duel and before he left to meet his opponent he would say to me, "Let's have spaghetti today." The remark meant that he was off to a duel. He used to say that fencing was for him a form of recreation. At that time his coach was the famous Ridolfi, who stood by him through thick and thin to the very last. Cirillo, the driver of the Alfa Romeo car which Benito acquired to replace the old open 1919 Bianchi he had kept until the March on Rome, used to race back home to give me the first news of the meeting. He generally limited himself to the curt remark, "We had a fight today and won."

His fiercest duel was with the Socialist deputy, Treves. Their mutual dislike was so intense that all efforts at reconciliation by friends had failed. After many violent passes, Treves got a nasty wound under the armpit. As usual my husband told me nothing of this meeting and all I heard about it was from our faithful Cirillo. Next day Benito went to Rome just as if nothing had happened and was there under arrest for a short time, as the result of incidents at a Fascist demonstration.

To describe minutely the various phases of the rise of Fascism prior to the March on Rome would fill a dozen volumes—the superficial story has already been told. I will say only that my husband was completely absorbed in planning the Party strategy. In the early autumn of 1922 he was already concentrating on the organization of "something exceptional", as he put it. His headquarters continued to be the editorial office of the *Popolo d'Italia* but sometimes he worked at home as well. From Milan and elsewhere came young men and their elders, war veterans and men still in the services, sometimes singly, sometimes in parties to take part in highly secret conferences. Time and again he was knocked up in the small hours of the night for urgent instructions. It was after one of these conferences that Benito confided to me that he had in hand "a very risky undertaking—a new, daring plan" and added that the outlook was "very promising". This was the first inkling I had of what was later to be called the "March on Rome". He used to tell me his secrets because he said I was a willing listener, did not ask stupid questions and showed an intense interest in his plans.

I surprised him time and again, by recalling minute details of past events which had escaped him or which he had forgotten, and it had by now become a practice for him to refer to me for names and places. He used to call me "a living diary" and one day he said, "Why don't you keep a real diary? It might be very useful one day." I protested that I had no time. But on second thoughts I was attracted by the idea that one day he and I might exchange notes on our lives in retrospect. So I began to keep a diary and in fact kept it religiously, with very few gaps, until the very last drama-packed days of the Italian Social Republic. More than once when it seemed advisable to have a written record of something, Benito used to say, "Take a note of that."

The first pages of my diary go back to October 1922. I think some of my entries preceding and during the March on Rome are sufficiently interesting to reproduce:

"10th October, 1922. Benito came home late tonight. I heard him come in because I'm a light sleeper, though he had been most careful not to wake me up and was most apologetic. Then he said he was glad I was awake so that he could talk about the schemes so dear to his heart. The struggle for power is growing fiercer every day and Benito is determined to bring it to a head, come what may. But supposing he's wrong and it's all a dream. What a blow it would be to him! No, that's impossible. He's too sure of himself. His strong will dominates men and events. He insisted on reading me an editorial he knocked off between calls tonight. His latest article always seems to me his best, but there'll be another, even more vigorous, tomorrow.

"20th October. Something new is in the air. Something big

is about to happen. Tonight Benito had just come in when some people came to fetch him. He must have been expecting them because he went out again without asking for anything. This waiting is nerve-wracking. If only there was no danger for him!

"23th October. I'm by myself. Benito left suddenly for Naples. He was in excellent spirits as he said goodbye. 'You'll see, Rachele, you'll see!' he shouted as he ran down the stairs.

"24th October. I waited for the phone call; I knew it would come. It was late afternoon when Benito rang up. He sounded very pleased and jerked out: 'All's going well, Rachele. I spoke at the San Carlo [Opera]. I'm quite satisfied. We are a sentimental people, but proud and really patriotic.' We were cut off before I could catch the rest. I share his satisfaction but at times the anxiety gets me down. I feel the crisis is at hand and am fearful.

"26th October. Benito has returned to Milan. Of the Naples speech he said: 'I tried to make them realize that our myth is the nation, the greatness of the nation, and not only territorially. I spoke to forty thousand Blackshirts and twenty thousand workmen. But at Naples I wanted to mislead our opponents. Now the time has come for us to act and we will act.' He was silent for a moment, as if apologizing for the worry he was causing me. Then, turning his burning eyes on me, he continued: 'We're all ready. We can't fail.' People stop me in the street and ask whether it is true that there is going to be a revolution. I reply that I know nothing, but I don't think I sound very convincing.

"27th October. What a day! Tonight Benito burst in on us. 'Hurry up and get dressed, Rachele. We're going to the theatre. We'll take Edda too.' I was dumbfounded. I know he likes the theatre but it seemed strange that he could think of amusement at this critical moment. There must be some explanation, I thought. He was certainly tickled by something, as he whistled cheerfully while buttoning his collar. A little later we three were at the Manzoni. He whispered: 'Use your eyes and don't miss anything, but keep your mouth shut.' I noticed that many opera-glasses were trained on him. 'The news has got round that the Fascists have mobilised,' he whispered again. 'We must pretend we know nothing about anything.' But that was easier said than done. There were repeated knocks at the door of our box and Benito had to go out. Fortunately the lights were out, and he could disappear, give his orders and slip back to his seat so as to seem absorbed in the opera. In the middle of the second act he suddenly rose and whispered, 'Now's the time, let's go.' He took my arm and we almost ran out of the theatre. At home there were many telephone conversations, one of them with a number of Fascists who pressed for authority to occupy the *Corriere della Sera* offices, the great daily which is openly hostile to the Fascist movement. Benito flatly refused, and asked me to give the same answer if the request was repeated. He was hardly out of the door before the phone went and there was a fresh clamour for permission to break up the newspaper. I repeated Mussolini's order.

"29th October. Benito was out all night. In the early hours the telephone rang non-stop. It was Rome calling. I heard a man's voice asking for Mussolini and answered that he was out but could be got at the *Popolo*. I was about to give its number when the voice said, 'He isn't there and we're very anxious to reach him. It's most urgent. It is the Palace calling.' 'But I don't know where he's gone.' A little later there was another ring. This time it was the Aide-de-Camp in person. He said he *must* know where Mussolini was. I did not know what to reply. Where could he be? Eventually Benito rang up. 'Yes, I've spoken to the Palace. Get my suitcase ready—morning coat and some linen. It's a matter of minutes. I've got to go to Rome at once.'

"30th October. He's gone. He came in to say good-bye and pick up the valise. He was in a great hurry. But he was triumphant: 'Rachele, the battle is won. The King has called on me to form the government. I'm glad he understood, and wanted to avoid bloodshed. Thank you for having encouraged and comforted me all these years without distracting me from my work. Now I need you more than ever. I know I'm a difficult husband but politics is like that. Give my love to the children.' A kiss, and he rushed down the stairs. When he had gone I could not keep back my tears. Not all tears of joy either. Benito's victory filled me with pride but I felt that the family had lost him. From now onwards he was the servant of destiny, which would raise him to the pinnacle of power. But the unknown, and much else, frightened me!"

From Rome, where he had made his headquarters at the Albergo Savoia, he started ringing me up every evening, a thoughtful practice he kept up whenever he was away from home.

Many newspapers and books have attributed to Mussolini

the well-known phrase: "Your Majesty, I bring you the Italy of Vittorio Veneto," on the occasion of his first meeting with the King. Truth requires me to say that to me he always denied that he ever said it.

CHAPTER IX

SIGNOR GIBUS

THE SCENES of Mussolini's first labours were the Palazzo Viminale, his office as the President of the Council and Minister of the Interior, and the Palazzo Chigi, where he functioned as Foreign Minister. The latter ministry had been transferred from the Consulta. His work was so heavy as to keep him away from me for long stretches. Our only "meetings" were the evening talks on the telephone in which he gave me his confidences and told me of the incidents, both amusing and annoying, which had filled his day. He used to say, "I've inherited a ship that's leaking everywhere and have found the officials incredibly slack; the functionaries of senior grades don't turn up until after ten o'clock."

He himself was always up before seven and got down to work at once. One evening in his first month of office he told me that he had literally turned the place upside down by going straight to the Viminale. "One day," he once told me, "I passed an usher on the staircase and asked him, 'Is there anyone upstairs?' 'Only that fellow Mussolini,' was the answer. 'He's always here by eight.' Then he recognized me and was overwhelmed with confusion."

We spent the summer season of 1922 in a modest *pension* by the sea at Levanto and went there again the next year, this time taking a furnished villa.

It was at Levanto that I received a magnificent present of flowers attached to which was a note, which at first completely baffled me, in these words, "Sent by the gentleman in the train who asks to be received." It was only when I invited the visitor to call that I recognized in him the other party in a curious incident which occurred in 1920 in a train during one of my journeys from Forli to Milan. I found myself taking part in a heated political discussion; the most fiery of the protagonists was a Genoese who was sitting next to me. He inveighed against

Mussolini and maintained that Fascism would never come to power. I preserved a deadly calm when I began to refute him but he kept on roaring and gesticulating wildly. "But do you know Mussolini?" I asked him. "Of course I do! And his wife as well!" We went on arguing but my quiet replies merely inflamed his irritation. Just before we arrived he wanted to introduce himself. Looking him straight in the face I decided to tell him the truth, "I am Signora Mussolini." It was the same man who came to Levanto to tell me that he had become a fervent Fascist.

One day while we were at Levanto a young pilot came down very low to wave to his fiancée who lived near the station. He got into difficulties and his aeroplane fell among the station buildings. At that very moment we were expecting the arrival of my husband who was coming by plane. Edda was a distant spectator of the accident and feared that something terrible had happened to her father. Running towards the scene of the disaster her suspicion became a certainty and we had great difficulty in convincing her that her father was not involved. But those moments of terror left her with a permanent aversion to flying, though she had previously travelled much by air, often under unpleasant conditions.

Benito's first separation from his family after his accession to power lasted forty days. During that time I went on living as before in Milan, though under more trying conditions. The circle of my acquaintance grew as if by magic, although there were few people I made any attempt to see. Among them was Princess Marianna Borromeo, a dear friend and assiduous caller. I was besieged by Italian and foreign journalists who came to interview me, and could not conceal their surprise at finding the wife of the President of the Council alone and immersed in the most humble household duties. I took good care not to make any sort of political pronouncements. I told them that I had nothing to do with politics and that I was Mussolini's wife—his wife and nothing else. Then I gracefully dismissed them.

This attitude of mine was the origin of what became the legend that I was completely disinterested in the official and political life of my husband. But the truth was quite otherwise in fact, as Benito continued to confide in me and, proud in this confidence and feeling myself the depositary of his aspirations and purposes, I decided to make myself the jealous guardian of everything he told me.

(*Right*) Benito Mussolini at the time he was attending the Instituto Magistrale where he trained as a school teacher

(*Below*) Benito Mussolini involved in a scuffle with the police in 1915 after they had broken up one of his meetings

The Mussolini family in 1927. Donna Rachele is holding her youngest son, Romano, Vittorio and Bruno are in front of their father, and Edda between her parents

Under the date 16th December, 1922, I find the following entry in my diary:

"Benito here on a visit. Very exciting day. He arrived incognito but the news of his arrival got round at once. The children and I had a wonderful time. Late at night, when we were alone, he told me a lot about his life in Rome, supplementing what he has said on the telephone. He described his first talk with the King, adding that he had been 'rather disappointed at his poor physique and his absolute lack of self-possession'. He said, 'I had the impression that everyone at the palace had his bags packed to get away from Rome before the insurrection. But the King understood and showed confidence, even giving me some words of encouragement. Now I am absolutely sure of his unconditional support. I have had a lot of trouble with some of the more ambitious fascists; success has gone to their heads and they're intoxicated with victory. They've become arrogant, advance claims of all kinds, foment quarrels and on the least difference of opinion join the opposition. They also fight amongst themselves and cannot be persuaded that after we have obtained power we must revert to the rule of law and make ourselves its advocates and defenders. While I should be occupying myself with the great international and internal problems facing Italy many of those who should be closely co-operating with me and relieving me of all the secondary problems are actually compelling me to spend my time on all the fiddling details and their personal disputes. As regards our enemies, they are quiet enough at the moment, but I shall have to keep an eye on them.'"

I remember how annoyed Benito got over court etiquette in those early days. Not that he was not at his ease—the story of lessons in deportment at court are just fables—but that he found it unreal and futile. (He also told me many years later that he was particularly irritated at having to turn up for royal audiences in a morning coat and top hat: "I believe three men are left who wear top hats—me, Stanlio and Ollio."

"17th December, 1922. Benito has given another day to his family. He has been playing with the children all the time. This evening he went to the theatre with Baron Russo (subsequently Marquis Paolucci di Calboli). He wanted me to come too but I had to decline as I had too much to do at home—I like satisfying his gastronomic preferences. There was an amusing incident at the theatre. After the performance was over the cloakroom attendant, apparently much moved, mixed up the

4

overcoats and gave the Baron's to Benito. Mussolini, careless
as ever, put it on and the Baron, equally absentminded,
accepted the President's. I saw Benito arriving home fuming
and perplexed: "Look at this coat, Rachele; it's frightfully
uncomfortable.' I took a good look and answered, 'But it's not
yours!' He took a closer look himself and burst out laughing.
The Baron was very perplexed but then laughed too and we
all had a good laugh.

"18th December, 1922. Benito at home and very happy. He
knows that the atmosphere here is much more congenial than
at the Viminale. He spoke of his recent visit to London, said he
was glad it was over and explained why. 'London is a nightmare
to anyone from Italy. All that grey grime penetrates everywhere, into your clothes, your room and even into your trunks;
there's no getting away from it; it's worse than the sand in the
desert. I hope I'll never have to go back to England.

" 'Good manners, all right, but nothing tangible, Rachele.
They don't or don't want to understand our needs. To them
Italy is small beer . . . but we'll change all that. If they want me
they'll have to come to Italy for me.'

"He also mentioned his journey to Switzerland and his meeting with Poincaré and Lord Curzon. 'They came to me,' he
said.

"He referred with satisfaction to the Lausanne Conference
on the settlement of the Middle East. 'The Dodecanese were
saved at Lausanne after I had opposed the proposal that the
islands should be handed over to the Allies. These gentlemen
are really too greedy—always in the name of the freedom of the
peoples, of course!' He said all this without the slightest heat,
no different from his tone when he was telling me his boldest
ambitions."

Benito's visit lasted about a week and we were all quite
miserable when he left, particularly because it was impossible
to say when we should see him again.

His next appearance was at Easter and I could hardly wait
for it. In my diary I find:

"He arrived this morning, rather tired but delighted to be
home among his wildly whooping children. We went for a
drive to Lake Como. At one point we stopped the car and got
out to walk down a lovely tree-lined avenue. Benito referred
again to the difficulties he was still meeting with among the
slack and slow-moving bureaucrats around him and then
turned to the problems of today and tomorrow: 'I've got to

build from the ground up! My projects are absolutely immense. I must revolutionize the social life of Italy. Every branch of public activity and production must increase and reach heights never touched before.'

"I listened in silence, fired with his enthusiasm and stupefied by such ambitions. At Brunate we met a group of tourists. One of the ladies, red-faced and out of breath, ran up to us: 'Do you happen to have seen Mussolini? He must be somewhere about as we recognized his car.' Benito looked the other way, and then we resumed our walk to escape an excessive and unwanted mobbing."

Although Benito had been in power only a few months he gave me innumerable examples of the positively fanatical enthusiasm he encountered. One man had repeatedly asked to be received in audience. When he was ultimately ushered into the presence of the President at the Viminale he was so overcome by emotion that as soon as he had blurted out, "I was determined to see you!" he fell to the floor in a faint. Another time an old police inspector, who had managed to get an audience, came to confess that he was the man who had once arrested him at Forli and even given him a beating. He actually offered him the very stick! It was an odd reminiscence which the President took in good part.

"It's quite incredible," said Benito, "the number of old soldiers who have come to life to tell me that they were among the comrades who carried me from the mortar pit to the dressing station when I was wounded. The number has now reached four hundred, though only some half dozen stretcher-bearers were concerned."

Even more surprising was the insistent importunities of friends and relations who asked—with varying degrees of discretion—for benefits and favours, and it was a tiring job to cope with them. Even some ancient creditors of Papa Alessandro turned up. One of them said that twenty-seven years before he had lent a cart wheel to the farm at Dovia and had never had it back! All these creditors, genuine or presumed, were sent away substantially satisfied.

When the summer of 1923 arrived we had another, though very short, visit from Benito. There is an entry in my diary for June:

"My husband was at the aerodrome for the Baracca Cup at Sesto Calende. On our way back he told me that in recent times the aerodrome had been almost deserted because our aviation was making no progress and hardly existed. 'I am devoting all my attention to rebuilding our air force. Aviation is the new weapon of war; it will decide future conflicts.' "

I think it was about that time that an incident occurred in which Cirillo was concerned—our faithful but ever-grumbling and not too bright chauffeur who was so kind to our children and was always surrounded by them. One morning Benito said to him, "Run down and bring up 'il gibus'.[1]" We had left it in the car. Cirillo stood pensive for a moment and then went off. The time passed and my husband began to get impatient. Nothing annoyed him more than to be kept waiting, as he himself was meticulously punctual. At length we decided to go down and see what Cirillo was doing. We found him standing to attention at the front door. "What are you doing, Cirillo?" "I'm waiting." "What for?" "Signor Gibus, sir."

It was during this visit of Mussolini to Milan that we arranged to have Edda, Vittorio and Bruno christened together by Don Colombo Bondanini, brother of Augusta, Arnaldo's wife. The latter, her husband and Manlio Morgagni were present at the ceremony. The very simple service took place at our house. In 1925 the children were confirmed, privately, at Camaldoli, near la Verna, by old Cardinal Vannutelli.

CHAPTER X

FOUR ATTEMPTS ON MUSSOLINI'S LIFE

FOR A long time I had been pressing Benito to visit Romagna, where he had not set foot for ten years. I kept telling him that I was being badgered with appeals for the Duce to visit his estate. These appeals had become urgent and at length he gave in. It was the summer of 1923. I will return to my diary:

"We travelled to Forli by special train and our first greeting was the ringing of all the bells. The streets were strewn with flowers and the crowd went wild with delight. We had hardly left the train before we were practically carried to the car waiting outside the station. When I was free of the throng and entered the car I found that my flowered hat in my hands had

[1] The opera hat, called after its inventor (tr.)

been reduced to a little unrecognizable rag. The crowd seemed crazy; they all wanted to get as close as possible, speak to Mussolini and win a nod of recognition. While the car was slowly threading its way forward amidst frantic cheering, Benito, deeply moved, exchanged a few remarks in Romagna dialect with the spectators nearest to him.

"After lunch in the palazzo of Marchese Paolucci di Calboli there was a round of ceremonies and speeches. In the prefecture I met the Contessa Merenda whose somewhat unwelcome tenants we had been when we first married. She was most enthusiastic. Milan, which boasted of being the Duce's adopted home, had sent its own imposing deputation in several hundred cars which paraded before us. It was on this occasion that the citizens of Predappio presented Benito with the house at Dovia where he was born, together with a scroll recording the gift."

The year 1924, a stormy one for us, brought me at short intervals a series of family disasters. First, my sister Pina, the mother of seven children, fell gravely ill. Her delicate health was quite unsuited to a hard country life. Her lungs were affected and the disease made headway. For three years I had been only too glad to give what help I could, even bringing her near to us in Milan in the hope that a more peaceful life would do her good. But, on the contrary, separation from her children made her even more unhappy. She was only thirty-five when she died, quietly and without pain but tortured by fears for the fate of the orphans, even though I had assured her that I would not neglect them—I never did (though they were not always grateful). My husband was very active in helping me. He was not able to be present at the funeral but asked me to lay a wreath in his name.

A little later, another of my sisters, Giovanna, mother of no less than fourteen children, died in childbirth. I find in my diary:

"They have just rung up to say that Giovanna's condition is very serious. Benito has only just arrived from Milan after a long absence and is full of ideas for his holiday, but when he heard of my sister's critical condition he personally urged me to leave at once. He is always very kind and understanding. Poor Giovanna! At any rate I should arrive in time to help her.

"When I got to Forli I had much difficulty in finding a car to take me to the house, thirty kilometres away. A tremendous storm was raging which forced us to stop several times and the hood of the car was beaten down by the hail.

I shall never forget my arrival at the stricken house, with the storm battering at the windows and all those innocent children crowding round their dying mother. My sister's state is really desperate: lack of medical attention has caused an infection and the great distances in the country has made immediate obstetrical assistance difficult. The poor woman's sole help has been her husband, who was then returning from the fields. I cannot recognize Giovanna, once so lovely and the picture of health and vitality, in this dying woman whispering feebly a prayer that I should not abandon her children. Her appeal met with an immediate response. I have already sent for a wet-nurse and shall adopt the little girl who is costing her mother's life. 'I give her to you with all my heart,' Giovanna said, and thanked me for all I had always done for her. At dawn next day my help was no longer required as Giovanna died. I am looking after the children and taking away the new born infant. My word is sacred.

"My little adopted daughter died this evening. I grieve as much as if she were my own child. I have done everything possible to save her."

The murder of the socialist deputy, Giacomo Matteotti, near Rome, after a dramatic kidnapping by fanatics, proved to be a great blow to Fascism itself and harmed no one more than my husband, who has often told me that it was a complete surprise to him.

In fact this was the beginning of a terrible time for Benito who had simultaneously to face the attacks of his enemies and order the necessary investigation and the arrest of the culprits and their accomplices, actual and presumed, some of whom were his collaborators. A large section of public opinion, both in Italy and abroad, was hostile. Cases of desertion and treason were not infrequent. His private secretary, Fasciola, went abroad and tried to sell documents presumed to be incriminating. A furious press campaign was unleashed, inciting revolt and revenge. Armando Casalini, the Fascist Syndicalist deputy, was assassinated by a person to whom he had done many a good turn.

I am not in a position to describe all the circumstances and incidents of that dramatic period of which I learned only from brief telephone conversations with my husband and the excitement among the public and in the Press. I know that Benito was extremely despondent. He often spoke to me of "formidable forces" against him. One evening he mentioned a *coup*

d'état engineered by certain ministers, headed by Luigi Federzoni, who wanted to compel Benito and his ministry to re-
sign.

A man who stayed close at Mussolini's side in this truly
critical phase of his struggle was Costanzo Ciano, whose un-
questioning, unshaken loyalty contributed enormously to keep
my husband on the path he had chosen. The man in the street,
generally speaking, and the Party leaders (among whom I
should mention Roberto Farinacci) alone remained faithful.
At that time, and also much later, Benito readily gave Farinacci
the credit of having "saved the situation" in this crisis.

As if all this were not enough it was during the Matteotti
affair that Mussolini had his first attack of stomach disorder,
the first real illness he had ever had since our marriage. It
was a great grief to me that I was so far away and could not
look after him myself.

By mutual arrangement with Benito, and indeed under
pressure from him (he was trying to cut down expenses), I
decided to move with my family to Carpena, near to my home
ground, where during the war I had bought a house and farm
with my savings and the legacy from my father, Alessandro. I
had done all I could not to change the pattern of my life,
but in a great city like Milan our new social position imposed
a certain minimum of obligations. At the same time, my
husband's residence in Rome involved other not inconsider-
able expenses he proposed to defray out of his salary as deputy
alone (he subsequently gave up that salary). I should be able
to live more cheaply in the country and so I left Milan, not
without much regret because I had been happy there, despite
many anxieties and sorrows.

I settled down very quickly at Carpena and took a great
liking to that country home, particularly as the children
were much freer there. My sole anxiety was the health of
my mother, which was beginning to deteriorate. As soon as
we arrived I sent Edda to the College of the SS. Annunziata in
Florence, because its solid reputation for learning promised
her a good education. Vittorio and Bruno attended schools
in Forli and also started cello lessons.

My mother's illness was not painful but most protracted.
My sister Rosa came to live with us to look after her. Mother's
affection for my children was almost a disease, as is almost
always the case with grandmothers, to whom grandchildren
are simply the children of children linked with them by a

double maternal tie. During the hard winter the invalid's condition became so much worse that she was unable to leave her bed at all. Another entry from my diary:

"1st November, 1925. I have been laying wreaths on Benito's family tomb in the cemetery of S. Cassiano. He has not been able to get away from Rome but is glad that I have been able to do this pious duty for himself as well. Then I went to Santa Lucia where my father rests. At home I found my mother a little better. 'I've been to take flowers to Daddy,' I said, though in the last few days she seemed to take no interest in anything. But she replied, 'Next year you'll be taking them to me. Look after Edda, Vittorio and Bruno; you must never fail them.' I was much shaken by her tone of quiet prophecy. She often said that her mother died on All Souls Day and that she herself would like to end her life on that blessed day."

Later she asked whether the boys had had their supper and at dawn next morning I found her stretched in the tranquil embrace of death. Poor, dear Mother! It seems that she went off to sleep happy in the thought that she was dying that day, as she had wished.

The boys looked on in wondering silence. It was the first time they had seen the sad sight of a human life drawing to a close. Edda did not get back in time to see her. Benito too grieved greatly because my mother had always lived with us. At that time he often telephoned me for news of the invalid. "I have to go to a ceremony," he once said. "Lots of people are ashamed of being called slaves, but who is more of a slave than I? Surely a home tragedy gives me some right to spare some of my time for my family?"

So I accompanied my mother to the cemetery with a few relations, in the midst of a large and respectful crowd.

On my return home after the funeral I was getting out of the car when I was told that the Marchese Paolucci di Calboli was on the telephone for me. He was my husband's secretary and it was quite exceptional for him to ring me up. He told me of Zaniboni's attempt to assassinate Mussolini. "The police discovered him in time. The Duce is safe," he assured me. I was inclined to disbelieve him but after a few minutes Benito rang me up himself, insisting that no importance should be attached to the incident and confining himself to the remark: "My luck's held once again." I badgered him for details but the only answer I got was, "The whole thing's quite unimportant. Tell me about Mother's funeral." I described it and then repeated my request for details of the attempted assassination. It was no use. He would not tell me any more. But this was only the first of a series of such attempts.

The death of my mother left a great void in our house and I found myself rather lonely. Benito understood my distress and agreed that when possible we should return to Milan, particularly as the children would be better able to finish their studies there, especially Edda who had been at the college in Florence for a year. With her lively temperament and independent character she had often championed the cause of the employees against the teaching staff, being rewarded with punishments she considered most unfair. When I went to bring her home the violin professor told me how much he regretted her leaving and the oldest of the employees wanted to kiss her on behalf of them all, such was their affection for the student who had suffered punishment in their defence.

Towards the end of 1925 Benito insisted on our going through the religious marriage ceremony. To me our deep attachment to each other, the fact that we had stood together as one in our stormy life together, and above all our children were a firmer bond than any conventions. But I readily agreed to consecrate our union in the sight of God.

The ceremony took place privately at Milan on 29th December. The witnesses, Arnaldo and the Marchese Paolucci di Calboli, were in a bit of a quandary as to whether the wedding should not be rather a grand affair, but I rescued them from their dilemma by telling them that it was an absolutely intimate family occasion. Monsignor Magnaghi, of the church of S. Pietro in Sala, conducted the service.

Apropos of marriage, I remember that Benito was strongly opposed to divorce. When our religious marriage took place, and on several other occasions, he said to me, "I will never allow divorce in Italy. The family is not an institution which can be dissolved at anyone's sweet will. There are definite social obligations. The religious injunction 'what God hath joined together let no man put asunder' is a wise safeguard for the family."

Barely five months after the first attempt on Benito's life there was a second, also in Rome. Once more Paolucci rang me up: "It's an Englishwoman, a poor old deranged fanatic called Violetta Gibson. Five revolver shots from very near, but luckily there is only one small wound, in the nose. The Duce remained utterly unruffled and went on with his work; he's just embarking for Tripoli." It was the evening of 7th April, 1926. I had my doubts whether Paolucci's story was strictly true as I feared that he was keeping something back not to alarm me. A wound in the nose; but how serious? I tried to telephone directly to Benito. It was impossible. I learned the details only towards the end of October when he asked me to accompany him to Bologna where the fourth anniversary of the revolution was being celebrated. Referring to the incident of 7th April, he remarked, "Though the Englishwoman did not kill me I was nearly killed by the doctors of the Medical Congress which I had just opened in the Campidoglio. In their anxiety to help me the illustrious scientists crowded round and almost suffocated me. I was horribly frightened, I can assure you. It was all I could do to defend myself very stoutly."

I was not actually present, though not far away, at the fourth attempt (the third took place at the Porta Pia in Rome on 11th September—a young anarchist threw a bomb which landed behind Mussolini's car) in Bologna on 31st October of the same year. I was in Bologna with Edda because Benito had asked us to be present at the ceremonies, which he said would be interesting. Among others there would be the opening of the "Littoriale", the great city stadium. Mussolini travelled to Bologna by car while we ourselves, with Arnaldo to accompany us, went by train. We had a wildly enthusiastic reception everywhere. Ridolfi, the fencing master who always followed my husband about, told us that during the journey he had mentioned to the Duce that he had some uncomfortable presentiment about a new attempt on his life. We guests lunched at the Prefecture while my husband was at the Casa del Fascio. There were thirteen ladies at the table and when I realized the fact I called out, "Thirteen at table! It means bad luck!" In the afternoon, after the close of the proceedings, I went to the station with Edda, accompanied by the Marchese Paolucci and the young wife of Attilio Teruzzi, who was an American. We stood about, quietly talking and waiting for Benito, who was to join us. There was a sudden movement in the crowd and we thought he must be coming. Instead, Paolucci, pale as death, came running towards us. He could not get a word out. His wife shook him to make him speak but he seemed to have taken leave of his senses.

Then, seeing me standing there he managed to say, "Courage, Signora, courage!" It was not his words, but what they implied, that frightened me. But at that moment Benito appeared in the middle of a crowd. Many of them were weeping and all were pressing round to get a sight of him.

As soon as he joined me he told me about the crime and how it had happened: "The procession was passing along in the ordinary way when I saw someone forcing his way through the crowd and approaching the car; I had just enough time to observe that it was a white-faced, shock-headed boy before he fired a small revolver in my direction. In a twinkling the crowd had him down and wreaked summary justice on him. It was impossible to stop them. It's monstrous to make a boy the instrument of a crime!"

CHAPTER XI

BENITO'S DAY

POPULAR REACTION to the latest attempt on Benito's life was so prompt and general that the incident was soon forgotten. Our train had to stop at every station, because the news had spread like wildfire and everyone wanted to see that the Duce was safe and sound. Ridolfi had tears in his eyes as he embraced Mussolini and reproached him for not having heeded his warnings. Mussolini got off the train at Imola to telephone to Bologna, and only then did he notice that his jacket had been singed. Later on, at Villa Carpena, we saw that the bullet had grazed his clothes and left a slight scratch in the region of the heart. We had a stream of visitors until late that night. When the Marquis Albicini anxiously inquired whether it was really true that he was unharmed, I pointed towards the inner room, whence came the sound of a violin. "Do you hear that? It's Benito." He was playing away, having forgotten all about his narrow escape.

We could not go back to our old home in Foro Bonaparte in Milan, so we settled into a six-room flat which my husband found in Via Mario Pagano. Arnaldo's family lived in Via Massena, nearby. The presence of my sister-in-law, Augusta, a good, kind-hearted soul, gave me the longed-for opportunity for a first visit to Benito in Rome, as I felt I could safely leave the children with her.

I had never been very keen on staying in Rome; I preferred to keep away from the political arena. Between the time the Duce left Milan to form the Government and Christmas, 1926 only once did I want to be with him, and my heart was set on it, but outside interference defeated me. It was in 1925, when he fell ill with stomach ulcers. I was not told about this for several days, but from the way he talked on the telephone I guessed there was something amiss. He admitted he was feeling unwell, but said there was nothing to worry about and my visit would be inexpedient for political reasons. When I became aware of how serious his condition was and tried to leave, the Milan Police Chief personally vetoed my going. Rumours that the Duce was very ill were already spreading throughout the country, and his colleagues believed, rightly or wrongly—I think wrongly—that my going to Rome would increase public alarm and have undesirable consequences.

I did not actually get away until Christmas 1926. I found Mussolini installed in a small flat in the Palazzo Tittoni in Via Rasella. It comprised a small entrance hall, a dining-room and four other rooms. The bedroom was the only decent sized room, but even there the lighting was poor. There was no room for a kitchen, and meals were sent up by Baron Fassini, who lived on the floor below. Housekeeping was in the hands of Cesira, a kind, forty-year-old spinster from Gubbio. She had come as a servant, gradually taken everything into her hands, and become something of an autocrat. Her zeal was unlimited, and she jealously resented any outside interference, even from me.

This Cesira appears to have been recommended to my husband by Signora Margherita Sarfatti, whose acquaintance he had first made when he was editing *Avanti!* Signora Margherita was a cultured, intelligent and domineering woman, slightly older than Mussolini and married to the well-known lawyer, Sarfatti. Their son, Roberto, who had won the Gold Medal (for valour) had been killed in the World War.

Signora Sarfatti had been art critic of the *Popolo d'Italia*. Being aloof and overbearing, she was unpopular with the staff and particularly disliked by Arnaldo, who was not unaware of her "sentimental" relations with Benito. She was chief sub-editor of the periodical *Gerarchia* and the moving spirit of the artistic movement known as "Novecento" (20th Century).

She wrote a book entitled *Dux*, about my husband, which he did not like. She was dismissed from *Popolo d'Italia* somewhere around 1930. Her relations with Mussolini were then at an end. I met her only once. She came to our house to call on Mussolini, then convalescing from the aeroplane crash. (She subsequently went to America and I have never heard anything more about her.)

In Via Rasella I met a few of Benito's colleagues. There was Aldo Finzi, Under-Secretary for the Interior, to whom I took an instinctive dislike, so much so that I even resented his sending me an enormous bouquet of flowers. He was dropped from the Government after the Matteotti crime and got mixed up in the scandal over compulsory rear-lamps on bicycles. (He was involved in the dramatic events which followed 8th September, 1943, and met his end as one of the victims whom the Germans shot at the Ardeatine Caves.)

I renewed my acquaintance with Paolucci di Calboli, the private secretary. He was a clever diplomat, always discreet, watchful and a hard worker. (This is the moment to mention the other private secretaries who followed Paolucci in this arduous and exacting post. The first was Alessandro Chiavolini, previously on the staff of *Popolo d'Italia*, who resigned because he disliked the idea of marriage—though he afterwards changed his mind. The next was Osvaldo Sebastiani, who kept the job longer than anyone else. He was removed because he was too easy with some of the Duce's meddlesome and greedy relatives and certain party high-ups. He had also built himself a much too imposing villa at Rocca di Papa which some people erroneously imagined was my husband's. Sebastiani was murdered by partisans in North Italy, in the presence of his wife and little daughter, during the period of the Social Republic. His successors were De Cesare, a civil servant, who lasted until 25th July, 1943, then, at Gargnano on Lake Garda, Prefect Dolfin, Cellai and the young Prefect Gatti, who was among the people shot at Dongo.

My first stay in Rome passed practically unnoticed. I deliberately avoided appearing at any public demonstration and even declined the invitations which I began to receive, especially from the Roman aristocracy when they found out that I was about.

Outwardly, Benito had changed. He dressed better and was meeting all sorts and conditions of men. But he was the same man at heart. Though extraordinarily busy, he planned his working day better, following a methodical system which, as he said, "helps to keep the body fit and the mind fresh". He rose at six and, after physical exercises, immediately drank an orangeade or a glass of grape juice. Then he went out for a canter and had a shower on his return. Breakfast consisted of fresh fruit, milk with a little coffee, and wholemeal bread when he could not get the Romagna bread I used to bake for him and which he liked so much. He had stopped smoking after the war. (I remember that the only time he accepted a cigarette was at the Valle Theatre, during the first performance of *Campo di Maggio* by Gioacchino Forzano, a play like *Villafranca*, in the writing of which he had collaborated.) He was in his office by eight, broke off a few minutes at eleven to eat some fruit and was back home at two. His meal invariably consisted of a little spaghetti with tomato sauce, fresh or cooked vegetables, a good deal of fruit, no coffee. Then into the study, where he went through the Italian and foreign papers. He even found time to study topical publications, when he was not engrossed in reading the classics. There was never any siesta. He was off to the office about six and back home about nine for supper, consisting of a clear soup, vegetables and fruit. Wine and spirits he never touched. Meals were a matter of a few minutes. He never lingered at the table or grumbled about his food, provided it was simple and natural. After supper he would drink an orangeade or camomile tea and went to bed about ten-thirty. He was always a heavy sleeper.

There was nothing smart about his clothes. His only fancy was ties—he liked them tasteful and of the best materials. He used eau de Cologne. Years before he had said there was only one thing he wanted: "If I could afford it, the only luxury I'd allow myself would be a change of bed linen every day." I obliged him as far as I could. And that was the only touch of "refinement" in our house.

My first stay in Rome was brief as I had to return to Milan to look after the house and children. Running the home was my department ever since Benito got one hundred and twenty lire per month on the *Lotta di Classe* and thereafter he always handed over his salary to me and forgot about it. He had not the slightest idea of what money meant and never had any on him even when he was head of the Government.

Edda, Vittorio and Bruno attended the State schools. Their father was adamant that they should not be "kept away from

ordinary people". On the subject of education, he used to
say that private schools "may further individual progress but
don't supply the most important part of knowledge, that
derived from living among children of every social category.
Contact with every type of human being improves character
and selfishness, innate in the young, is automatically checked".

These ideas show that Mussolini did not change at all after
he came to power. He continued to prefer simple living. He
never favoured formality in family affairs and had neither
the time nor inclination to give presents. The only present I
received before his advent to power was a gold bracelet with
spiral bands. And even that was mainly prompted by the
example of his brother Arnaldo who had presented his own
wife, Augusta, with an identical article. Mussolini gave me
the bracelet with an air of triumph, expecting me to wax
enthusiastic over it. But I disappointed him by saying that I
wanted no jewellery of any kind—nor have I wanted any
since. I have never possessed jewels or valuable furs, except in
the imagination of scandal-loving newspapers. The only fur
coat I ever had was the one I bought for eight hundred lire
during the last war, and which has now been confiscated.

CHAPTER XII

THE "CONCILIATION"

I MET the Queen Mother, Margherita, only once, at Milan,
a few months before her death. My diary entry is as follows:

"I took the children to the Sports Palace where the film
'Life of Christ' was being shown. Queen Margherita was there
too, and received a great ovation. During the performance her
aide-de-camp came came over to me and said, 'Madam, Her
Majesty the Queen invites you to go to her box with your
children.' I was somewhat embarrassed at the prospect of
meeting the royal lady face to face, but once in her presence,
my nervousness vanished at the sound of her sweet voice.
'I have been looking forward to meeting you, signora, and
making the acquaintance of your children,' she said, and proceeded to inquire about their ages and what school they
attended. 'I have often asked your husband about them, and
I know that Edda is intelligent, and very lively,' she continued,

stroking Edda's hair with her white, well-shaped hand. 'You must be proud of your husband, and the House of Savoy should be very grateful to him for his hard work. I am an admirer of your husband and feel confident he will govern the country well. He interests me greatly. Anyone who loves music must have a very fine mind, but I can't imagine how he finds time to play the violin.'

"The Queen kept us with her for about half an hour. I was fascinated by her personality. She is a queen in every sense of the word. Her kind feelings towards Benito touched me deeply."

Very shortly afterwards she fell ill and died. She appointed my husband executor of her will. King Victor Emmanuel handed Benito a small ancient medal that Queen Margherita had always carried about with her; it was her express wish that it should be left to Mussolini. (He wore it around his neck until his death.)

In that same year, 1927, I found I was going to have another baby—after ten years. Benito was delighted and kept saying, 'I want the boy—we were certain it was going to be a boy—to be born in the Romagna. He must be a 'romagnolo', like his father and grandfather before him."

So I went off to Carpena. Just before the child was due, I wired my husband in Rome, because he had made a great point of being informed in time. He arrived within five hours, proud of his feat. "I've never driven like that before," he said. He handed me a layette, with the remark that the new arrival would be the first to use it. He brought with him a big bundle of telegrams from abroad, a rumour having prematurely spread that I had given birth to a boy. He showed them to me, amused and yet a bit worried. "They should have gone to Stefani[1] but I stopped them. It's got to be a boy now."

Romano was born on 26th September. At dawn, a servant carrying the new arrival in her arms, woke Benito. He rushed in at once to congratulate me, and I could see he was more moved than he cared to show. I had reserved a surprise for him—the gift of a little farm at Carpena which had been bought with the proceeds of the publication of his articles in America.

The birth of Romano was celebrated far and wide. A vast number of congratulatory telegrams arrived from all quarters. Our rooms were filled with flowers and gifts, some of them of great value. Low-flying aeroplanes swept over the roof of our

---

[1] Stefani—The official news agency.

house, dropping flowers, gifts and messages in the garden. Ferrarin, the Italian ace, sent a medal with the effigy of the Madonna of the Airmen. A gold watch was presented by a Spanish aviator, and American airmen sent a lot of flowers. Marquis Paolucci planted an oak tree in the garden which later prospered mightily. Shortly afterwards a case arrived from America with layettes and trousseau from birth to six years of age. Actually it was so richly stocked that it would have sufficed for a dozen children. A small golden statuette of San Romano with a precious relic was sent from Rome. And every province contributed its quota from local arts and crafts. Had Romano been able to keep nothing else but these gifts, he would have been well off all his life. But my husband and I agreed that they should nearly all be given to charity.

"You are the sea that receives water from all quarters only to give it back to all the rivers," I said.

To celebrate the event, on 27th September the Italian Navy lit the big revolving beacon on the Rocca delle Camminate tower. Right up to the beginning of the war its flashing light swept the Romagna plain, the Adriatic and the most distant Appenine peaks.

As soon as I could get about again, I threw myself heart and soul into the business of looking after our estate. We children of the Romagna all have a passion for the soil. At Carpena I started the systematic breeding of poultry and other farmyard stock. Acquiring new specimens was my hobby and I used to spend hours reorganizing the runs and houses and improving the farm buildings. My experiments used to amuse and mystify Benito but the only animals in which he was really interested were horses.

Now that our financial position was better and I could do more for the poor I could extend the welfare work in Milan which I had started within my then limited means when Benito was editor of *Avanti!* To recall all my activities in this connection would be impossible, but I well remember how I used to like to go by train—an ordinary fare-paying passenger —and mix with people of all sorts and conditions. Unrecognized by them, I would listen to their conversation, try to understand what they needed and then see what I could do to help them.

Meanwhile, on the national level, Mussolini was doing more and more for the working classes with his "Labour Charter" and much social and welfare legislation. He used to say to

me, "Workers must be secured against exploitation by employers, though the standing of the employer must be preserved.
Every section of production, every branch of labour, must be
looked after, whether skilled metal workers, farm labourers,
women rice-pickers or miners. They must be given welfare
services, comfortable homes, medical facilities and entertainment after their toil." By the summer of 1927 the "Battle for
Grain" was in full swing.

The title of "Duce" which the Fascists had unanimously
bestowed on Mussolini before the March on Rome was now
being universally adopted by Italians and even abroad.
Socialist comrade Olindo Vernocchi had coined the phrase
"our Duce", back in the days of Socialist struggles in Forli.
I myself began calling Benito "Il Duce", even with members
of the family, and later on our grandchildren called him
"grandpa Duce".

To me the word was no empty formula. I had always tried
to be a useful and loyal colleague of my husband and I redoubled my efforts as I began to realize how the Italian
people's expectations were mounting together with Italy's and
my husband's prestige. He could not be everywhere at once,
know everybody's needs and keep an eye on what all his
associates, high and low, were doing, particularly in remote
areas, so I tried to see what I could do, especially in the
Romagna. During the summer season I made a point of
visiting the farthest corners of Forli province. I made my
way up valleys as far as the Apennine watershed and got to
places which the authorities rarely visited, if ever. I often had
to ride a mule where there were no roads—they were built
later—in order to bring essential relief to places so neglected
that the inhabitants sometimes even lacked salt.

Before the conclusion of the Lateran Pact of Conciliation
between the Church and the Italian State, I had had vague
and occasional hints from Benito himself that negotiations were
in progress. I knew about the meetings with Cardinal Gasparri, the activities of the two sets of representatives, and the
recent frequent talks between my husband and the lawyer
Pacelli. It was none the less a surprise to me when Benito
telephoned from Rome to tell me that the agreement had been
signed on the 11th February, 1929. That evening I had received
a visit from Father Facchinetti, a friend of ours, whom I had
known for some time. He was a Franciscan with an attractive
personality, and later was appointed Bishop of Tripoli. The

news was already known in town and he was beside himself with joy. He gave us his blessing, and exclaimed, "This is the holiest achievement of our time, the most important event in the history of Catholicism since 1870." While Benito was on the phone, Father Facchinetti insisted on congratulating the Duce there and then. Speaking into the receiver he said, "You have every reason for satisfaction: you have solved a problem which was too much for statesmen like Cavour and saints like Don Bosco."

During that same year occurred two domestic events affecting our lives considerably. I myself announced the first to Benito: I was expecting a fifth child.

"It must be a girl this time," he immediately replied, "three boys must bring a girl."

And a girl it was whom I gave birth to at Carpena. My diary has the following entry dated 3rd September, 1929:

"Anna Maria was born at 1 p.m. She is a beautiful, bright-eyed little creature. We had not agreed on a name beforehand but when Benito arrived from Rome, and told me he had already thought of calling her after my mother, it was a delightful surprise. He had actually given the name to the Stefani news agency already. Each new child fills Benito with tenderness and joy. He has also told me that at last he is looking for a suitable home where we can all live together in Rome —'I want really to enjoy my children in my spare time.' He described several villas which were offered by their owners as soon as his wishes were known. But so far all have various drawbacks, some of them pointed out by the police. While Mussolini was alone he did not mind where he lived but now that he wants us with him, he knows there are certain essential requirements."

At the end of October he informed me he had found a suitable place. It was the Villa Torlonia, offered to him time and again by Prince Giovanni Torlonia himself and where he had previously lived at certain periods. The Villa, a handsome building in the neo-classical style, in the Nomentana quarter, is thrown pleasantly into relief by the luxurious greenery of a magnificent garden. The extensive grounds include other buildings connected by avenues adorned with statues and obelisks. There is a pond surrounded by lawns and clumps of trees over-topped by tall slender pines.

Our move to Rome on 15th November was the second great event of the year. After the first few days my diary records:

"We have been in Rome for a fortnight, but there is still much to be done to adapt our new home to our requirements, modest though they are. The park is very suitable as a quiet and secluded retreat for my husband. It is full of inviting nooks and abounds with all kinds of trees and shrubs. There are large hot-houses, a small theatre and a little villa to which our host has retired. He seems really glad to have us in his home and goes out of his way to make us comfortable. Prince Torlonia is the perfect gentleman."

CHAPTER XIII

VILLA TORLONIA

THE NEGUS HAILE SELASSIE had been received by Mussolini at Villa Torlonia before we made it our home. It was during the Negus's visit to Rome, that the Duce presented him with an aeroplane—a gift that was very much appreciated.

It can now be revealed that the idea of developing Abyssinia with Italian labour was born during that very visit. I remember Mussolini telling me, in the early days of our moving in, that he foresaw "a great future for Italy in Abyssinia" and had found the Negus "a clever and cultured man, with whom I believe we shall get on very well".

Like every "Romagnolo", Benito was passionately fond of music and a great enthusiast for the theatrical season. Sometimes we also used to attend film showings at the Institute for Cultural Relations Abroad, and even have cinema shows in our own house. Opera was by far his favourite entertainment, but he was much too busy to go to the Royal Opera House, though he rented a box every season and paid the ordinary subscription. The box was mostly used by Vittorio and Bruno who on several occasions met Queen Elena and the Princesses in the foyer. The ladies used to treat my boys with great kindness.

Apropos of Benito's interest in the theatre, when we were living in Milan and he was editing *Popolo d'Italia* he often asked me to go with him to some particular play. If I was too busy with domestic duties, he would take my mother. The company of our maid was also welcome. He would get terribly impatient when the performance was late in starting or the interval too long, and he once frightened my mother by making as if to take off his shoe and throw it at the curtain. He enjoyed Petrolini's performances immensely and had a very high opinion of the artist's remarkable powers as actor and mimic.

Benito never stayed long at home. Most of the time he was busily working at Palazzo Venezia, when he was not travelling. Yet we spent many happy hours together at Villa Torlonia with our children, and later, with our grandchildren. He cherished those hours so jealously that he was positively annoyed one day when some American cameramen, after persistent badgering, extorted permission to make a documentary film of home life at the Villa Torlonia. Some scenes had to be repeated over and over again. He was obviously restless and fidgety and objected to the dazzling light of the arc lamps. On that occasion he expressed his amazement at the powers of endurance of movie "stars".

He rode horses and bicycles in the grounds and always enjoyed playing out-door games with the boys. He was good at tennis and often complimented by well-known players. I rather objected to his playing football with the children as broken windows in the veranda were the usual result. He liked spending the more restful hours indoors at cards, skittles or billiards.

He was fond of animals, especially horses. Some of these were splendid specimens, such as Ned, a bay, April, a chestnut, which was given to him by some English friends, and magnificent Fru Fru, which he rode at Tripoli on the occasion when the Mohammedans presented the Sword of Islam to him. Benito often gave his horses lumps of sugar and once, to my dismay, he used this bait to entice Fru Fru up the front steps and into the house. (Some of these horses were stolen after 25th July, 1943.)

There were always plenty of dogs at the Villa Torlonia. The favourite was Charlottino, which lived to fourteen. A huge old cat belonging to Prince Torlonia was frozen to death one hard winter. Another cat, of a most valuable breed, was given to us by an English lord. Then there were the wild animals presented by various donors. After keeping them at the Villa for a time, Benito used to send them to the Rome Zoo. Two lions, Ras and Italia, gave birth to three cubs with which our children occasionally played. Edda brought a jaguar from Brazil. Benito had a puma on a leash in his room for some time. We had to send it away because it managed to get loose one night and caused a panic by wandering through the house. A great royal eagle was kept in the garden. There were Coco the monkey, a deer and two gazelles, a gift to me during a tour in Libya. The gazelles produced a baby which the children, for some unknown reason, christened Jupiter Jovis; its parents died but it defied the climate and its environment as it had been born in captivity. Once during a snowfall we thought we had lost it but it reappeared after a few days, emerging from a barn where it had taken refuge. We also had a falcon, some small parrots and canaries, Bibi and Bobo the tortoises (which Benito disliked) and two graceful ponies which were another present from England to Romano and Anna Maria.

Benito and Costanzo Ciano had been very close friends for many years. This friendship was greatly strengthened when the Admiral proved his loyalty to my husband at the time of the crisis which followed the Matteotti crime. In the course of time this mutual affection spread to the two families, and in 1930 our firstborn, Edda, became engaged to Ciano's son, Galeazzo. She was then only eighteen but he was not her first suitor. Some time before the engagement there had been a brief idyll with the son of Orsi Mangelli, the Romagna industrialist. The pair met during a tour in Spain and our holidays at Riccione. After supper one evening the young man lingered on and seemed very embarrassed. He finally plucked up courage and asked my husband if he could talk to him alone. Red in the face, he suddenly asked about Edda's dowry. "Dowry?" replied Mussolini in amazement. "My daughter has nothing at all, and neither have I."

The candidate for Edda's hand went off and was not seen again. As a matter of fact, we afterwards learned that it was his father who had insisted on his sounding us first and his action had been deeply regretted by his mother and his paternal grandfather, who was a great gentleman.

My husband entirely approved of Edda's engagement to Ciano and the marriage was fixed for 24th April of that year. We arranged a reception, and I find the following entries in my diary:

"The Villa Torlonia is smothered in white flowers; it looks like a huge hothouse. Though I was not responsible for organizing the reception, I have found myself making all the arrangements. I can hardly believe that Edda is really getting married

—she is still so young. Up to now her temperament has been more like a boy's. A keen sportswoman, vivacious and self-willed, Edda does not seem to me sufficiently ripe for marriage yet. The wedding is to take place in two days' time."

Prominent Italians and foreigners and all the diplomatic representatives were present at the reception. It was a distinguished gathering and I recognized many well-known faces. I tried to watch them without appearing inquisitive. I particularly noticed the Russian Ambassadress, who was literally smothered in jewels and wearing an expensive fur coat, as if she were determined to remind us of the distant Russian snows in the sunshine of our mild spring weather.

"Flowers and presents poured in in an endless stream. The servants told me they didn't know where to put the flowers, so they have been stacked in four lorries, to be sent to the church and the Tomb of the Fallen at the Verano Cemetery.

"Before the reception we had a photograph taken in the garden. There was myself, Benito and our five children. Anna Maria fidgeted in my arms and smiled at the photographer. This photograph will be our last souvenir of Edda as a girl, with her short hair. (She has never bothered about hair styles.)

"24th April, 1930. The parish priest performed the marriage ceremony in the Church of San Giuseppe in the Via Nomentana. Witnesses for Edda : Prince Torlonia and Under-Secretary Dino Grandi. All the outstanding figures in Italian politics, as well as the relatives and friends, were present—four thousand in all. But I could not take my eyes off Edda's pale face, looking at her with a mixture of affection and grief, as I knew that I was losing her, or at any rate all but losing her. All her girlhood came to memory. I could see her as a small tot, the only consolation of our restless life. I found myself unable to pray to the many Madonnas smiling at me from among their niches and all I could say was: Lord, may she be happy. Benito too was much moved. I could tell by the way he knitted his brows. More than once his eyes caught mine, and we exchanged an understanding glance."

After a few months Galeazzo was appointed consul at Shanghai and the young couple left for China. It was a sad parting for Benito and me. As the years crept on, he had become ever more deeply attached to his elder daughter, who resembled him in so many ways. News from the couple was slow in coming, and waiting for it was a dreary business. In 1931, however, I met Guglielmo Marconi at the marriage of

Galeazzo's sister, Maria, to Mr. Magistrati. Marconi had a pleasant surprise for me:

"I'll soon have you talking to your daughter at Shanghai," he said.

Never have I blessed the practical application of genius so much as the day that the great inventor enabled me to speak to Edda. I knew my daughter was about to give birth to her first child, and being able to communicate with her across thousands of miles was a great consolation. A few months later—it was 1st October, 1931—Benito rushed into my room with a telegram in his hand: "We're getting old, Rachele, we're grandparents already!" he said. "What!" "Yes, Edda has a boy, Fabrizio."

I knew everything had gone off all right, but distance prevented my being with the young mother to look after her and the tiny creature of whom I knew nothing but his name.

Benito had a very special concern for the needs of the region where he was born. On one of our trips to the Romagna that year we stopped at the Instituto Magistrale[1] building in Forlimpopoli, where my husband had finished his studies and graduated as a teacher. No one was expecting him, and he decided to pay a surprise visit. His entrance caused amazement, alarm, confusion—the sort of panic which Benito's unexpected appearance anywhere always aroused. He saw some of his old teachers, made the acquaintance of later arrivals and before leaving went round the lecture rooms he had once haunted as an intelligent, if difficult pupil.

He said nothing on our way back. I too kept my thoughts to myself, and this, as usual, inspired him to confide in me:

"Didn't you notice what a state those rooms are in? How can professors looking as shabby as that teach their pupils order and hygience?"

It had occurred to me that Benito must have spotted the teachers' shoddy, unkempt appearance. He brought up the subject again that evening, as he always did when there was something on his mind. "That's settled!" he exclaimed with a satisfied air. His solution was that the teachers should be provided with some sort of uniform.

"We'll create the right atmosphere, where the premises and the teachers themselves are the personification of order, so that the pupils will automatically learn to respect the school."

On another visit to the Romagna we called at Monte-

[1] Training College.

maggiore, where the Mussolinis originally came from, about ten kilometres from Predappio. Benito flirted with the idea of buying back the old farm where his forebears had lived, but the owners demanded too high a price of lawyer Zambelli, who acted on our behalf. My husband thought he could not afford it and confined himself to a request, willingly granted, to be allowed to put up a memorial tablet on the old farmhouse. He wrote the inscription himself:

FROM 1600 TO 1900
ON THIS FARM CALLED COLLINIA
GENERATIONS OF MUSSOLINIS
LIVED AND WORKED
AND HERE MY FATHER WAS BORN
ON THE 11TH NOVEMBER 1854

The day the tablet was unveiled, Benito gazed at it long and happily, as if it had been a nobleman's ancient escutcheon of which he was intensely proud. It was on this occasion that he visited the old parish church of Montemaggiore. It was in such a pitiful condition that he had a new church built. I myself laid the first stone some time later.

On the day the tablet was unveiled, we found a nine-year-old girl, totally blind, living in the farm. It was a very sad case, and we immediately arranged that the child should be taken to Florence for an examination and then treated in a clinic. Here she began to improve and one day we received a touching letter from her father telling us that she had completely recovered.

December 1931 witnessed a most unusual reception at the Villa Torlonia. It took place in our private cinema, where a concert was given in honour of Mahatma Gandhi. To the amazement of the "gentry" who had been invited, the Mahatma turned up with his inseparable goat on a leash. There was an extraordinary and strange fascination about the Mahatma, and his manner was kind and gentle in the extreme. After the reception, Benito made the following remarks amongst other comments:

"He is a holy man, a genius, and unique in that he uses goodness as a weapon. Perhaps he is one of the few people in the world who really understand the British and their imperial policy. If India ever becomes free, she will owe it to this man . . . and he tells me he is sure of liberating his people in his own lifetime."

CHAPTER XIV

DEATH OF ARNALDO

O<small>N AN</small> autumn day in 1928—I do not recall the exact date but it was while I was still living in the Via Mario Pagano at Milan—I was called to the telephone. It was Arnaldo speaking and he was in a terrible state.

"I'm speaking from the doctor's," he said. "I've brought Sandrino, and the doctor says there's no hope."

Sandrino was then about twenty, a pale, thin, intelligent and rather shy youth, with fine features; the eldest child and his father's darling. He was also a quiet lad and something of a dreamer. He had shown signs of physical exhaustion for some time and we were extremely worried. The doctor had said that the trouble was hæmophilia, an incurable illness. The distracted father revealed the doctor's terrible verdict to no one but myself.

Sandrino got worse during the summer of 1930, in spite of everything we could do. He was then living at Cesenatico. My husband hurried to his side to take a last farewell. The dying youth asked his father to have him buried in the small cemetery of Paderno, near his mother's house, where he was born. He died on 20th August. It was a terrible blow to my relatives. Arnaldo, normally a mild-mannered man, often worked himself up into sudden rages, railing at the untimely fate which had prematurely deprived him of his beloved son. The bereaved father's heart suffered a shock from which it never recovered.

The presence of Sandrino continued to haunt his father's house and inspired Arnaldo to write a book in memory of his dead son. The intense feeling in this book touches sublime pathos. The boy's personal belongings were preserved with religious respect; even his place at table was left empty. The room he had occupied became a sort of shrine where a lamp, never extinguished, shone on a huge portrait which seemed to bring him back to life. Servants did not stay long in that lugubrious atmosphere.

We made Arnaldo come to live with us in Rome in the hope that he would leave behind the sad memories haunting his own home, but he brought his sorrow with him and his health began to deteriorate. Then came the first heart-attacks. We

got him the best medical attention but the patient's changed
looks and tragic expression made us feel the task was hopeless.
His thoughts of death were linked with a fanatical hope of
rejoining his dear son.

Benito, who had kept no secrets from him, tried to shake
him out of his apathy with cheerful, vigorous advice, while I
concentrated on coaxing him to let himself go and unburden
his mind. I also kept a close eye on his health, which he was
neglecting. I was extremely fond of him because he was a
model of goodness and rectitude and much attached to Benito.
He was readier to confide in me, as he always felt rather dominated by his brother. To him Benito was more the Chief than
a brother.

After some time, Arnaldo decided to return to Milan. On
the day he left I said to Benito as we sat at table, "Arnaldo
has only a few days to live."

Benito looked up sharply and replied, "That can't be; he's
quite well."

But obviously he was far from sure. I myself had talked to
the doctor, who had confirmed the sad news.

On 21st December, 1931, which was very cold, I went for
our usual drive to Ostia with Benito and Anna Maria (he
generally went part of the way on his motor-bicycle). On the
way back I left him at the Palazzo Venezia and proceeded
home, making a long detour because the baby was asleep and
I did not want to wake her. As we approached Villa Torlonia,
I noticed a number of cars parked outside. I felt a sudden
shock, and quickly got out with the child in my arms. I saw
Arpinati, Under-Secretary for the Interior. "What's the
matter?" I cried.

"Dreadful news," he replied brokenly.

"Is he dead?"

"Yes, he's dead."

Barely stifling a scream, I rushed upstairs. Dropping the
child on the nearest couch, I frantically searched the first-
floor rooms, believing that Benito was dead. I found him
at last—safe and sound, but overcome with grief. Only then
did I sense that it was Arnaldo who was dead. I clasped my
husband's hands, realizing how great was his loss.

It was a dreadful sorrow for him: he had always valued
his brother's loyal and devoted work. Only when Arnaldo
was no more did he come to know how much he had loved him.

We immediately left for Milan where, during the night

before the funeral, Benito watched over his brother's body in the lying-in-state at the offices of *Popolo d'Italia*. The funeral was most impressive. In the Romagna too, there was universal mourning when the coffin was borne to the quiet cemetery of Paderno where Arnaldo was buried, as he had wished, next to Sandrino. Benito subsequently published his brother's story in a book entitled *The Life of Arnaldo*. It contained a colourful and moving record of their boyhood together at Predappio.

One problem remained: who was to be editor of *Popolo d'Italia*? My husband was too busy with the problems of government, though he confided to me that at the bottom of his heart he would have liked to return to his old battle station. He eventually decided to appoint Vito, Arnaldo's second child. When he sent for him he said, "No one but a Mussolini shall edit the paper. I'll help you when necessary, but you must be the editor."

I always had an aversion to Court ceremonies, with their formalism and rigid etiquette, and nearly always managed to find some pretext for declining the frequent invitations I received. Benito used to say with a smile, "You're the only woman who says no to royalty." Altogether I went only twice to the Quirinal Palace. My diary has the following entries, under May 1930:

"Went to Court today. The sort of prim solemnity that dominates the proceedings is not to my taste. Despite the formal smiles, everybody seems to be quickly taking stock of everybody else and one can sense the repressed rivalries, jealousies and spite. The King came up to me and drew my attention to a group of elderly ladies-in-waiting, whose *décolletés* were very daring, though their shoulders could hardly be called junoesque: 'Look at that; outsiders all speak admiringly of Court ladies, but I feel as if I were surrounded by hens.' We both laughed."

On the second occasion, Benito was asked to take me to a performance at the Quirinal on the occasion of some treat for the little Princess Maria. I was nursing Anna Maria at the time and my husband asked that I should be excused on that ground. The Queen insisted, however, and assured him that she would let me go in good time. I went to the Palace and noticed that Her Majesty glanced at her watch from time to time. When the three hours' interval between feedings was almost up she sent me off, giving me a rose. While saying good-bye, she confided to me, as one mother to another, how worried she was about the little princesses, whom she did not like leaving entirely to governesses. She said that she was in the habit of listening at the children's bedroom door during the night to make sure they were all right.

The year 1932 was a great one for the régime, a year of mounting popularity for Benito. The tenth year of the Revolution was celebrated throughout the country and an exhibition commemorating the Fascist rise to power was opened in the Palazzo delle Esposizioni. It was an enormous success and made a great impression on foreigners as well as Italians. The land reclamation plan was in full swing and marking up its first great success with the draining of the Pontine Marshes. New towns sprang up and large-scale public utility schemes were starting and public buildings rising in every province. Mussolini was delighted and proud of the success of what he described as "these great works of civilization".

I should like to say something about Mussolini's relationships with women because I have a greater right than anyone else to express opinions on the subject. But my memory of him as an affectionate father and husband prompts me to greater indulgence than has ever been accorded to him, alive or dead. So I shall confine myself, as I have done hitherto, to a few notes in order of time.

Benito dearly loved me, his home and his children. Such a statement does not interest anyone looking for "romance", but it is the plain truth. His affection for me never changed from the moment when, swept off my feet by love and his passionate threats, I threw in my lot with him. Fifteen lire and our youth were all we had when we set up house. He was unfailingly kind and considerate to me, and always valued my common sense. Our characters were so akin that we never needed lengthy explanations—a few words would suffice. I knew his tastes and was therefore able to anticipate his slightest wish. Indeed, we both had the same simple tastes; these never changed, even when fortune smiled on us. One day when our grandchildren's nurses in their sumptuous uniforms were gathered together in the park at Rocca delle Camminate, Benito remarked, as he sat down on some steps: "Only we two never change."

Another bond between us was our overwhelming love for Italy. It was my feelings on that subject which made me understand what he was working for, and devote myself to seeing that he was not disturbed in it. (I believe that our tragedy might have been less had his efforts met with more understanding and support from some of his associates; it was certainly unnecessary to go to extremes to bring my husband down.)

My habit of silence led him to confide in me, even on the most important subjects. He used to say, "I like to know you're there, at my side, a steady influence, because you're a pillar of strength."

His activity was incredible. His meetings, journeys, reading, home life and sport, left very little time for gallantry. I do not deny that he had some love affairs, but the fanatical devotion he inspired made them readily comprehensible, and he was always the first to tell me about them. Sometimes his contrition was positively comic.

Once at Riccione, as he ran into the sea for a swim a bevy of women—young and not so young—threw discretion to the winds and rushed into the water after him. Many of them were fully dressed, and I still remember the scarves and bags floating about. Three girls in danger of drowning were rescued just in time.

When I went out in Rome, or visited the Romagna, especially the Predappio district, I was usually engaged in welfare work. I could see by their warm reception that the peasants were genuinely fond of me. For a long time I continued travelling by train as an ordinary fare-paying passenger, so as to mix freely with my fellow men. I too had some amusing, though brief, encounters with enterprising lady-killers. During a trip from Rome to Bologna I was pestered by the attentions of an admirer who insisted on forcing his visiting card on me, and was very outspoken in expressing his feelings. When we reached our destination, and the traveller saw the impressive reception I was given by the Prefect, who was waiting for me at the station, he finally grasped the situation and was covered with confusion.

CHAPTER XV

THE EMPIRE

AFTER MY husband recovered from his stomach trouble, the Royal Family pressed him to use certain rooms in the Castel

Porziano as a flat and gave him the run of the royal estate. Benito never occupied the flat, but after 1930 he frequently spent some of his very few leisure hours in the magnificent pinewood that stretches down to the sea near Ostia. He also used a hunting lodge and for the exercise often joined a party for pigeon shooting, though he was not very keen on hunting. Later on I too went for walks on the royal estate with my children and had a wooden hut built, which was more comfortable than the lodge. I have always liked hunting, my only recreation.

On 17th–18th March, 1933, the first meeting between Ramsay MacDonald, Lord Simon and Mussolini took place. It was in Rome and its purpose the working out of the Four-Power Pact. My husband always had kindly feelings for these two welcome guests, and my diary for 18th March records some of his impressions:

"The British Government seems at last to understand the necessity for a revision of the treaties. MacDonald's views and mine are almost completely identical. He realizes that Italy is no longer the country she was in the immediate post-war period. I am grateful to him for this, and for his welcome cordiality."

We spent the summer of 1933 partly at Riccione and partly at Rocca delle Camminate. The latter was a castle which the province of Forli had presented to the Duce some years previously. It had been completely restored on the old foundations and in the same style. We gradually furnished it and it became our favourite home during the summer season and Benito's favourite retreat when he needed a rest at other times of the year.

Rocca delle Camminate is very ancient and has a long history of wars and sieges. The origin of the name is uncertain; it belonged to the Malatestas, the Guidis, and many other fighting gentry down the centuries. The interior was very gaunt and simple, and my husband's big study was on the ground floor. Below the high, narrow windows let into the thickness of the walls were stone benches. The library was well stocked. There was a small parlour with leather screens decorated with oriental designs, and Japanese furniture, a gift from the Mikado. There were also several *objets d'art* presented by Chiang-Kai-Shek. On the next floor were the bedrooms. Benito's was a spacious, though simple, corner room, with massive furniture of some dark wood. A terrace intersected by passages enabled one to make the circuit of the castle, which was surmounted by battlements in the Guelph style. Here we felt at home and quite at our ease, with the splendid view of the great Romagna plain falling away to the Adriatic. On the flanks rose the Appennines, with the three peaks of San Marino in the distance. We gradually collected at Rocca most of the gifts my husband was continually receiving from every part of Italy and the rest of the world.

On the Duce's birthday, 29th July, folk dances were sometimes held in the courtyard of the Castle and Benito enjoyed them, just as he enjoyed the singing of the Romagna choirs, because the whole thing was absolutely informal. These homely jollities, unfortunately few and far between, went on far into the night with the help of the moon or floodlights and ended with the traditional fireworks which he greatly admired. In the evening he sometimes played "Napoleon" patience. At other times films were shown and he particularly enjoyed the comic ones. They seemed to bring him some relief from his many preoccupations.

He often used to take the children bicycle rides in the vicinity and these jaunts, with no police at his elbow, were often marked by amusing and touching episodes. One day Benito walked into a peasants' cottage, the home of a poor and very large family, and found its owner arguing with a bricklayer about adding a small room to the building. Money was the stumbling-block because the bricklayer needed too much material. My husband, who had entered unobserved and was listening to the discussion, suddenly broke in:

"How many bricks do you need to build this room?" When the amazement and confusion had gradually subsided the builder repeated his figures. My husband, whose past experience stood him in good stead, made some adjustments in the calculation and handed out a certificate for the number of bricks actually required. "Then you'll need a stall for the cow," he continued and started taking measurements.

So the room was built and the stall as well and eventually the whole house was done up. The peasant even had beds for the children and some other furniture.

In June 1934, Mussolini had his first meeting with Adolf Hitler, the head of National Socialist Germany, who had the highest regard and admiration for my husband. (In Hitler's study in the Brown House at Munich there was nothing but a portrait of Ferdinand II and a bust of the Duce.) That first

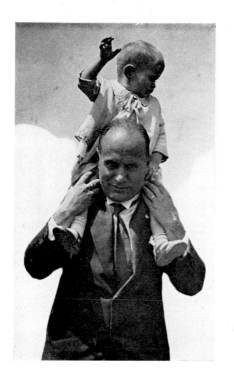

Mussolini family pictures: (*above left*) Benito and his youngest son, Romano; (*above right*) Vittorio and Bruno on a Mediterranean cruise; (*right*) Mussolini and his daughter Edda at Forli

Playing the violin was one of Mussolini's favourite relaxations

meeting took place at Venice, in the Villa di Stra, but its outcome was unsatisfactory. Mussolini told me, "Hitler talked a lot, often tumbling over his words, and put forward some wild ideas. He hasn't much self-control. Our meeting came to nothing."

So Benito obviously came away with an uncomfortable feeling, though there were some common interests which suggested a close union between Italy and Germany against the policy pursued by the League of Nations. The Austrian question was the main bone of contention. In this connection Benito used to say, "It is not in Italy's interests, and contrary to her wishes, that the adjacent republic should be absorbed by Germany."

It is now known that when the murder of Dolfuss made the threat of the *anschluss* much more urgent Mussolini reacted promptly by sending some divisions to the Brenner frontier, a gesture which was then sufficient to halt the German plans. What is not known, however, is the fact that Mussolini was extremely disappointed that the Western Powers stood aside and left Italy unsupported and isolated. At dinner one evening my husband remarked with obvious irritation, "I expected more from our Western friends, Rachele. They've let me down. Their apathy could have been disastrous." This may explain why, when these same powers asked Italy to intervene again, under very different circumstances, the *anschluss* could no longer be prevented.

Against the crumbling old wall of the Rocca there was an old almond tree. Though threatening to fall, even the builders engaged on the restoration had respectfully left it intact. It seemed to be withering, but Benito took pity on it, pruned it and banked it up with earth, and the next season it blossomed again. It made him as happy as a child. He often used to chop wood and rope us in to cut the grass in the meadows sloping down the Rocca. He was equally fond of long talks in Romagnolo dialect with peasants, farm labourers and other country folk.

But the hours of ease were always being interrupted by the cares of government and urgent international developments.

Between Benito and Dolfuss, the head of the Austrian government, there was a strong bond of friendship and mutual esteem. My husband personally made inquiries about a suitable villa near our house in Riccione where Frau Dolfuss and her two small children could spend the summer of 1934 and enjoy the bathing. I well remember the day—26th July, 1934—on which Frau Dolfuss was rung up by her husband and told that he was leaving Vienna for Riccione. Their little girl was rather seriously ill and the mother was anxiously waiting for his arrival when we received the news that the Chancellor had been assassinated in his office.

Someone had to break the news to the widow, and the sad duty fell to my husband. As always on such occasions, and in his sorrow and embarrassment, he asked me to go with him. A violent thunderstorm was raging at the time. Helping each other and trying to soften its impact, we broke the sad news to Frau Dolfuss. She decided to leave for Vienna immediately and the Duce placed an aeroplane at her disposal, with an Austrian police officer as escort. I learnt subsequently that she met with a hostile reception from all her relatives. She came back looking quite changed and much older, yet she remembered to bring the Duce the ancient key of the city of Venice which was kept at Vienna and Dolfuss had intended to present to him. She also brought presents for me and our children and a personal letter from Dolfuss committing his family to Mussolini's care. Some time later she and her children left for the United States, where I believe they are still living.

In January 1935, while the European situation was still tense as a result of the melancholy Dolfuss affairs, Pierre Laval met Mussolini in Rome.

"It's a question," Mussolini told me, "of solving the Ethiopian problem in the spirit of the Four-Power pact." When the meeting was over Benito gave me a general survey of the position which I carefully noted in my diary:

"Laval, who is undoubtedly one of the ablest French diplomats, fully understands our claims and is doing all he can to prevent Italy being isolated. We have reached an agreement. Italy will carry on her work in Ethiopia while opening the door to emigration. The development of Abyssinia—and the rest of Africa too, for that matter—is in the interests of Europe as well as Italy. Italy's peaceful penetration in Ethiopia is permitted by the Laval agreement and constitutes a major contribution to European peace."

Before leaving, Laval sent me a splendid bouquet with a note in the friendliest terms towards Italy. Unfortunately the agreement did not fulfil expectations, for reasons which are now history and no part of my story. To Mussolini this came as a blow to national pride. As he was always saying, "The

problem of our surplus population has got to be solved somehow," and he found himself compelled to choose the alternative
of using force to secure what he had done his best to obtain by
peaceful diplomacy.

An event which the Press regarded as critical occurred in
June—the meeting with Anthony Eden. By then the relations
between Italy and England had become so strained that the
talk could hardly be held in anything else but, in Benito's
words, "a chilly atmosphere with no place for cordiality.
We felt we were enemies, I temporarily, but he a sworn enemy
of Italy."

Preparations for the colonial enterprise in East Africa gathered momentum day by day. Diplomacy was out of the ring.
Arms would now decide the issue. Vittoria and Bruno, both
as keen on flying as their father, wanted to learn to fly. The
first to get a civilian pilot's licence was Vittorio. I find an
entry in my diary on 24th August, 1935:

"Today we said good-bye to Vittoria and Bruno. They
left for Naples, where they embark for Africa. Bruno has
been attending a flying school for months and wanted extra
training because he was afraid he might not get his licence
in time to join up for the war as a pilot. Flying school training
is not enough; there is an age limit. The minimum for volun-
teers is eighteen, and Bruno was sixteen only a few months
ago. Special authority was needed and Bruno nagged at me,
his own mother, to induce his father to get him accepted. I
hesitated for a few days before I decided what to do.

"Fancy such a request coming from you," Benito replied
when I tackled him. I made no reply but just looked into his
eyes and we understood each other. Ultimately the delighted
Bruno was able to don the smart uniform of a sub-lieutenant
(Air).

"2nd October, 1935. Crowds gathering in every town and
village of Italy to hear the expected announcement of the
declaration of war against Ethiopia. I left Rocca and went
down to Predappio, mingling with the stream of peasants and
workmen pouring down from the surrounding hills into the
piazza, where we listened to the Duce's speech, relayed from
the balcony of the Piazza Venezia. The ringing of the church
bells summoning the countryside echoed through the valley,
mingling with the lusty singing of the crowd in the piazza.
Wars can hardly be said to be popular; but the war which is
starting today has gripped even the humblest imagination."

"20th October, 1935. Things are going well. Adowa is behind us and the advance continues. I have never seen my husband so sure of himself and his plans. When the capture of Adowa was announced we gave ourselves a very exceptional treat and toasted the event with a glass of champagne. When I got back to Rome from Rocca the other day he came to meet me and said, 'Don't worry, Rachele, it'll be alright,' almost as if he meant to forestall the question he had read in my eyes, because there are some doubters, and even defeatists, about. The word 'sanctions' is being bandied about in certain very worried circles.

"12th November, 1935. Geneva has come out with its sanctions but my husband is as optimistic as ever. 'You can be quite certain,' he said today as he read the latest telegrams from Geneva, 'that we shan't run short of bread or petrol. Our plans have already been laid.' But there are many glum faces too—not in the working class, but in the middle class circles and even among the Party leaders."

The Duce devoted himself to the prompt despatch of the men and materials required to ensure the speedy success of the operations. I remember an occasion when the well-known Professor Castellani, appointed head of the medical services in Africa and finding himself unable to secure the despatch of certain men he considered indispensable through the normal bureaucratic channels, came to enlist my help. I put him in touch with Mussolini, and the necessary action was taken forthwith.

I had no inside information about the progress of operations in Ethiopia, because I have never concerned myself with technical matters and as a rule my husband never talked about them. He used to give me the news of our two sons which was wired to him from the front every day. He also hung up a big map of Ethiopia in the hall of the Villa Torlonia and used to spend a considerable time moving the little flags indicating the battle-line according to the latest war communiqués.

On his return, Bruno told us that whatever might be said about others he and Vittoria invariably lived and messed only with officers of their own rank and did not curry favour with superiors.

"18th November, 1935. I laid my wedding ring and that of my husband on the 'Altar of the Fatherland' this morning. We bought them during the hard times at Forli, though there had been no marriage service. They had cost thirty lire each. Benito handed me his ring with a wistful smile and the remark, 'what memories in this little yellow circle!' I also brought along one pound weight of gold and have sent 300 lb. of silver, together with a large number of the gifts made to the Duce over a considerable period. My husband has also given orders that the metal parts of other gifts are to be melted down. This will apparently yield several tons.

"What a sight the Piazza Venetia was this morning! The Queen got there before me.

"9th May, 1936. Today has been the climax. An atmosphere of indescribable enthusiasm pervades our house. Every single Italian seems eager to show his gratitude to the Duce. An avalanche of letters and telegrams has descended upon us. Late yesterday afternoon the Court sent Arborio Mella di Sant'Elia to bring me a huge bunch of roses from the Queen with her compliments and flattering references to the Duce.

"I was still under the spell of my emotions as a little earlier Mussolini had proclaimed the establishment of the Empire to the vast, delirious throng. I was anxious to hear my husband's speech myself, so I went to the Piazza Venezia and mingled with the crowd. I took Romano and Anna Maria with me.

"After supper this evening Benito told me about his meeting with the King at the Quirinal. Victor Emmanuel suddenly got up and said, 'Mussolini, as a reward for the Ethiopian victory will you, in addition to my personal congratulations and the gratitude of our country, accept the title of Prince for yourself and your descendants.' 'Your Majesty,' answered the Duce, 'I wish to remain plain Mussolini, as I have always been.' The King, now Emperor, replied, 'But a peerage at least.' 'The Mussolinis have always been peasants, and I am rather proud of the fact,' was my husband's answer.

"I fully approved of my husband's attitude. The refusal was no empty gesture. It was the only answer that he, a man of the people, could give. 'The King,' Benito went on, 'was puzzled at my resolution. But all that matters is that the war has ended well and the people are satisfied. Now I shall be able to welcome my sons home.'"

I cannot close this chapter without emphasising the fact that the Ethiopian campaign marked a turning point in Italian foreign policy. Not because we gained an Empire, but because our neighbour, Germany, had backed us. As the struggle swayed to and fro Mussolini more than once received letters and telegrams of encouragement from Hitler. I think he read most of them to me and often said, "It's strange that Germany, with whom we did not want to commit ourselves, is the very country to help us, while others with whom we wish to keep on friendly terms stand in our path."

It is true enough—and Benito would often stress this point as proof that the Italian cause was a good one—that many private individuals, British, French, North and South American, and of other nationalities, sent us messages of encouragement, but the only great power to oppose sanctions was Germany. Her "wooing" during a critical period paved the way for the successive international marriages which led up to the developments of recent history.

CHAPTER XVI

OUR CHILDREN MARRY

TWENTY-FIFTH MAY, 1936. How strange the Italian people's reactions to the proclamation of the Empire have been! Yesterday my husband gave me a pile of letters which had come in from every part of the country. They were written by people of every class and walk of life, and all harped on the same theme. Here are some excerpts, taken at random: 'Duce, you have given us an empire and we want you to be its head. It is yours. You are entitled to it. It has been conquered in your name. Your strong will has forced the hand of destiny and that hand will still point the way.' 'In the name of the people we implore you, O Duce, to make yourself supreme head of the nation you have raised to such heights. It is the wish of all of us: the negligible minority which is not with us consists solely of the parasites of the dynasty, an outmoded institution which is doomed to extinction. It is you we want to follow. You must be our leader. With you as our head we shall preserve the glory and the fruits of victory.'"

I gave the letters back to Benito with the remark, "I too have received a lot of letters to the same effect. They want you as Emperor!" "One is one too many," he replied. "If

Tafari hadn't bolted I'd have let him stay on. I even thought of making him King of Ethiopia or Shoah, with an Italian governor at his side. Progress isn't just a matter of abolishing institutions overnight."

Apropos of correspondence, I might mention that I was subjected to a daily bombardment of letters, mainly petitions, requests for help and charity. Four clerks of the Duce's private secretariat were employed solely in opening, sorting and answering them. More than ten million were received over a period of twenty years, and were duly filed and dealt with. "You must be the most written-to woman in the world," Benito used to say. When Arnaldo died, there were so many telegrams and letters of condolence they had to be taken away in lorries. For quite a time I had to meet personally the heavy cost of excess postage on letters insufficiently stamped. And I take this opportunity to repeat that my husband had long since waived all emoluments due to him as Prime Minister, the head of several departments and a deputy. It was always his ambition to cost the nation nothing, and we always lived on his salary of thirty thousand lire from *Popolo d'Italia*, the proceeds of articles he used to write for foreign papers, especially American, and the return from our landed property.

I was overjoyed when Vittorio and Bruno came back from Africa and settled down at home again. Vittorio, however, left shortly after. He had developed a keen interest in the cinema and wanted to visit the Hollywood studios. Bruno's hobby was flying and he took part in international races and outstanding events such as the Istrès–Damascus–Paris circuit on 26th August, 1937, and the Rome Rio de Janeiro transatlantic flight by the so-called "Green Rats" squadron in which he joined Colonel Biseo and Captain Moscatelli. He came to say good-bye just before taking off. All I said—I come from the Romagna where folk are shy of showing their feelings—was, "don't go too fast!" "Think of me with a snail on my plane," was his reply.

The proclamation of the Empire ended many months of tension, and there followed a period of tranquillity at home such as I had rarely been able to enjoy and which I dreamed could be prolonged indefinitely. With the victorious conclusion of the Ethiopian war Italy enjoyed a position in world affairs never attained since the Roman Empire. I wanted my husband to withdraw from public life, and constantly urged that course on him during the spring of 1936, "it may well be that your political mission is finished; you should think of yourself and your family a bit." But he invariably replied, "No, Rachele, we must press on. I feel there's still so much to be done, particularly in the way of social security and consolidating our victories. You keep your mind on the home." He looked on himself as a soldier on guard. To him relinquishing the responsibility of government was tantamount to abandoning his post.

He often told me that his objectives were: to develop the newly-won empire; to carry on the battle against the swamps; extend and increase the benefits of social security; to make the Italian economy independent at last and to foster art, which was the glory of Rome.

He was intensely interested in the draining of the Pontine Marshes. Being sceptical about the official reports which, as he used to say, were "artfully designed to prove the existence of non-existent results", he asked me to do some checking myself and tell him, for instance, whether certain rows of trees had actually been planted, or whether certain buildings had really been roofed.

His misgivings about official reports increased when our children began to mix with ordinary folk and come into contact with individuals prepared to speak their mind. Their experience during the war had made men of them and they had shed the diffidence so characteristic of the Mussolinis, especially during boyhood. They were quite ready to talk, especially Bruno. As an officer in the Air Force, he had no hesitation in drawing our attention to certain embellishments of the truth on the part of the High Commands. During meals he would often say, "They're keeping things back. We're only seeing what they want us to see."

Our family suffered another blow, which almost ended in tragedy, during the summer of 1936. Little Anna Maria, who was growing into a strong, healthy child, went down with whooping cough. I sent her to Tivoli with her brother Romano, for a change of air, and there she developed a far more dangerous disease. She began to have headaches and then came high temperatures. Eventually Dr. Salaroli told us the dreadful truth. It was poliomyelitis. Terrible weeks followed, and the entries in my diary are scanty, as I never left the child, day or night. But the frantic anxiety of that terrible crisis still haunts me. It was a very serious case, as her arms and legs were attacked. Her condition rapidly deteriorated. Benito sat by her bedside for hours on end as our darling hung between life and death. We relived the awful days we had known when Bruno was so seriously ill, with the same sleepless nights and grim vigils.

"2nd June, 1936. Still no hope. Benito is worn out. He was deeply shocked by Anna Maria's cry, 'If I can't move for the rest of my life, I'd rather die.' Poor little thing! Yet she's the one who questions the doctors and talks of her illness with an unaffected simplicity that makes us shudder.

"8th June, 1936. Some little hope now, but shall we ever see our Anna Maria walk again? Yesterday, the window suddenly blew open and Benito shot up, shouting, 'Shut that window or the wind will carry off my child.' There's no greater fighter in a political battle, but he can't cope with the cruelty of illness when it strikes his children and Anna Maria won't let anyone be with her except me and her father.

"10th June, 1936. Galeazzo brought some urgent official telegrams. The Duce received him in the room next to Anna Maria's. The Ethiopian question has to be dealt with at the League of Nations. 'They might leave me in peace at my child's bedside!' I heard him shout. This is the first time he has found the business of government a burden."

Anna Maria was attended most devotedly by Professors Valagussa and Ronchi as well as Salaroli and Serena, who were all greatly impressed by her strength of character. Kind messages, and even medical advice, poured in from all over the country. A Japanese doctor took a great interest in the case and an American scientist sent a special serum.

"12th June, 1936. Professor Valagussa has told me a shocking story. There is a family in Rome in which three children were struck down by paralysis; two died, the third went blind and the father became mad with grief. Since yesterday Anna Maria is a little bit better. Is she going to recover?

"20th June, 1936. Anna Maria is saved! Just when the doctors had given up all hope. A miracle? We all think it is."

Convalescence was long and very trying. When Anna Maria got up, we had to take her for carriage drives through the garden of Villa Braschi, where we were staying. She enjoyed playing with the toys which came in vast numbers from all quarters. Queen Elena sent her a beautiful talking doll.

Vittorio was married on 6th February, 1937. When Bruno heard that his brother had got engaged to Orsola Buvoli, a Milanese girl, he had tried to make Vittorio change his mind, because the two brothers were inseparable and he did not want to lose his boon companion. But Bruno was soon in love himself and finally decided to tell his father that he wanted to get married. I, of course, was well aware of what was brewing; mothers are always the first to know of their children's love affairs. The girl who caught Bruno's fancy was Gina Ruberti, the daughter of a Roman official.

It was an amusing scene. Bruno, usually so forthcoming, seemed tongue-tied. All he managed to blurt out was that his fiancée came from a good middle class family. His father listened in silence, then looked him squarely in the face and rapped out, "And who do you think you are?"

Bruno burst out laughing, realizing that he had secured paternal approval, and the conversation turned to other matters.

Bruno was married on 29th October, 1938. The procedure was much the same for both weddings. There was a reception at the Grand Hotel, and the religious ceremony was held at the church of San Giuseppe in the Via Nomentana, in the presence of a vast congregation. My sons wore their Air Force uniforms. The brides' white dresses and long trains made them look even younger than they were.

I found the ceremonies very moving, as my sons were hardly more than boys and I still looked on them as such. I had warned the brides that they might find the name of Mussolini a bit of an incubus. Benito was proud and happy. He would have liked to keep the young couples at the Villa Torlonia, as was the patriarchal custom in the Romagna. It was left to me to dissuade him, pointing out that young people like to have their own homes and no interference. "But the house must never be empty," he retorted. Ultimately he saw my point and gave way.

The wedding presents were most remarkable. The Prince of Piedmont, who had given Vittorio a tea set which became famous because one of the cups was broken, sent a golden set this time. Bruno received many gifts from abroad, where his flying exploits had made him better known. They included *objets d'art* and even race horses. From Japan came very valuable jewellery.

Bruno had purchased a small villa, which he was paying for by instalments, out of his salary. His friends vied with each other in furnishing it, and Colonel Biseo's sister, who was an artist, did the interior decoration.

CHAPTER XVII

THE PACTS ARE BORN

ONE AFTERNOON, just about the time when we were making preparations for Vittorio's marriage, Mussolini said, "Rachele, I've decided to help the Spanish Nationalists. I've been thinking it over for a long time; there's no alternative. Bolshevism in Spain means bolshevism in France, which means bolshevism next door and in fact a serious threat to bolshevise Europe. Franco's a tip-top general and I firmly believe his country has its part to play in the Latin world. I'm convinced he'll win." I put forward the woman's usual argument, that to us war can never be anything but a very sad necessity, but he smilingly insisted: "I repeat that Western civilization, the true European civilization, is in danger; so is Catholicism and the balance of power in the Mediterranean. We're not asking for Spanish territory in return for our services. We want the bolshevist effort in Spain to be crushed, so that it won't spread over Europe, including Italy."

Italian aid to the Nationalists was prompt and, according to Benito, "decisive". With a great show of the artful and devious ways of diplomacy, Mussolini succeeded in getting large supplies and thousands of men to the Spanish front, despite the maritime blockade. His preoccupations with the war and its international reactions were intensified by his concern as a father, as Bruno decided to volunteer for flying service in Spain. We tried to calm our fears by hardly ever talking about him, though the news of Bruno's presence in the Spanish National Air Force soon reached the other side, which began making special efforts to shoot him down. In fact, Generalissimo Franco urged the Duce to recall Bruno and the latter returned to Rome, after taking part in twenty-seven actions.

With affairs of state weighing increasingly heavily upon him, my husband began to find relief in his interest in his grandchildren, whom he adored. First came Edda's children. We found Fabrizio already quite a boy when his parents returned from abroad. Then came Vittorio's and Bruno's little brood, Guido, Marina and Adria, all about the same age. We were extremely fond of them. Now that they are all so far away, the aching void they have left makes me realize still more how much I loved those youngsters who bear Mussolini's name and have inherited his features.

We had wonderful times whenever their children visited ours. Benito would have liked them around the whole time. They often came over during the week, and on Sundays there was always a family gathering. My diary records many little incidents which gave me more pleasure than all my husband's political successes.

While the Spanish war was still in full swing, Hitler and Mussolini had their second meeting, at Munich and Berlin during September 1937. To understand the background, it should be remembered that since the first meeting at Venice, we had gained an empire, in the teeth of Geneva's opposition and in part, thanks to Germany's steadfast and solid support.

The Duce was going to Germany for the first time to meet the head of the German State, with the very object of demonstrating Italy's gratitude for that support. The Germans in turn showed their deep appreciation of this act of courtesy, and reciprocated by giving him a rousing reception all along the line, culminating in a huge mass meeting in Berlin, where Hitler and Mussolini solemnly proclaimed the two nations' friendship. He rang me up to tell me about the ceremony and said that after the very first evening he had been "surprised and greatly moved by these people's demonstrations of friendship".

After his speech at Berlin, which he delivered in perfect German (my husband also spoke English, French, Spanish and knew Latin), he telephoned me to ask whether I had been listening, adding:

"There's marvellous organization here and a nation of exceptional virility, quite determined to dare anything and everything."

It was during these meetings that Mussolini and Hitler laid the foundations of what was subsequently to be known as the "Pact of Steel" and, on the international level, provided for Italy's adhesion to the Anti-Comintern Pact which followed almost immediately.

On his return from Munich and Berlin, Benito gave me a circumstantial account of his visit, the magnificent welcome he had received and the fantastic demonstrations in his honour. He told me he had been "particularly impressed" by German organization and their war machine . . . "It's a marvellous machine; the smallest cog works perfectly." But he did not omit certain amusing incidents which had showed that there can be a hitch even in the most careful preparations. Here are his actual words: "During the military review the mace bearer was too quick and struck a soldier behind him on the head, and an artillery horse kicked over the traces and bolted right in front of the box. Hitler laughed and so did I. Then he turned to me and remarked confidentially, 'I don't like to think what'll happen to that wretched private. Our perfect German organization will be set in motion. The general will go for the colonel; the colonel will go for the major; the major will go for the captain; the captain will go for the lieutenant; the lieutenant will go for the sergeant-major; the sergeant-major for the sergeant, the sergeant for the corporal, and finally . . . poor private!' "

On the serious side, Mussolini told me about the purpose of the Anti-Comintern Pact and the Pact of Steel. I carefully recorded his words in my diary, which reads:

"We are trying to create a firm anti-bolshevik front in Europe, stretching from the North Sea to the Mediterranean. The Fuehrer and I have sized up the Muscovite move in Spain in exactly the same way. It can be said that Spain has given us our first opportunity for a vigorous plan for common defence against bolshevism. We shall make every effort to extend and strengthen this defensive system. But defensive it is, as I see it, with no immediate military objectives and there is nothing aggressive about it. If we could build up a bloc of nations that really matter, I think it would be enough to induce Moscow to confine its field of action and experiments to its own nationals."

He also spoke to me of "the Latin world" and "the centuries of civilization which are the living heritage we must defend". As regards the new relations between Italy and Germany, these are his exact words: "Germany is a great power and she realizes that the other great power in continental Europe must necessarily be Italy. Geographically, they together hold the vertical centre of the continent; Latin-world and Germanic-world will have met and they will defend European and Christian civilization against all bolshevik and atheist infiltration."

Nineteen hundred and thirty-eight witnessed two historic events which were the outcome of the new orientation of Italian foreign policy—the proclamation of the *Anschluss* and Hitler's visit to Rome, Naples and Florence.

When German troops marched into Vienna on 11th March, Mussolini was privately much shocked, as it meant a decisive step towards destroying the European New Order which the Duce had in mind in the Four Power Pact. He told me of his anxieties. "I still regret the break with our former allies, Rachele. But Germany's formidable military power is a new factor and history marches on, whatever men may do or not do. What has happened today might have been avoided if our Western friends had appreciated my gesture four years ago. Europe must unite; and it would be ideal if it would unite peacefully. But there's too much opposition, too much red-hot nationalism and so European unity can only come about through military action. I hope, and I shall go on hoping, that I may be able to limit military action to the minimum required to convince the heads of the European governments that Europe must unite, in both economic and political senses into one solid *bloc*, which can be the only real defence against bolshevism."

There are few Italians, and probably few foreigners, who do not remember Hitler's visit to Rome, Naples and Florence at the beginning of May 1938. The courtesies extended to Benito during his trip to Germany had to be reciprocated, and the visitor shown that the Italian people, in Benito's words, "is strong enough to defend Latin civilization."

The new station at Ostia was rushed up in record time, and the streets of Rome were decorated and brilliantly illuminated. Hitler was particularly impressed by the floodlighting and fireworks at the Colosseum, and almost fell out of his car in his efforts to get a better view. At Naples the navy gave a demonstration of its solid power which my husband told me was flawless, adding that Hitler came away in no doubt that Italy was worthy to stand side by side with Germany.

In the interests of truth, I must add that Hitler's visit was the occasion of a delicate situation as regards relations between the King and the Duce. My husband confided to me that Hitler wanted to stay with him, having no great liking for Victor Emmanuel. But Mussolini impressed upon him that the conventions must be strictly observed. So the Duce respectfully kept in the background during the celebrations in Rome and Naples, giving the King the place of honour. While in Rome, Hitler was the guest of the Quirinal, not Mussolini's, and several times openly betrayed his boredom with what he described as "the poor hospitality offered at the Royal Palace".

I remember, for instance, that he disliked the food at the Quirinal and found it "pretty bad".

Indeed, it was only when he was alone with Mussolini at Florence that Hitler recovered his spirits, and it was at Florence that the leaders of Fascism and National-Socialism were entirely at their ease, strengthening relations between the two countries in the intervals of visits to the artistic masterpieces which Hitler so much admired.

The awkward situation which arose during Hitler's visit was not the first of its kind. There had been a previous case after the proclamation of the Empire, when the Chamber and the Senate, jointly deliberating on a proposal put forward by Costanzo Ciano and Emilio de Bono, decided to confer the title of "First Marshal of the Empire" on both the King and the Duce. The King, so Benito told me, made no secret of the fact that he was very annoyed. To avoid making the King's resentment worse, my husband very rarely wore his First Marshal's uniform, and hardly ever when the King was present.

Notwithstanding these contretemps, which Mussolini referred to as "in a minor key", the Royal Family showed their high regard for Mussolini on many occasions. Shortly after the proclamation of the Empire, Prince Umberto visited the grave of the Duce's parents and the house where he was born at Predappio. The King himself made the same pilgrimage and was our guest at Caminate on 8th June, 1938, soon after Hitler's visit to Italy.

I remember that it was a red-letter day for us. When we saw the procession of royal cars winding round the bends of the road leading up from Predappio to the Rocca, I and my husband walked down to welcome the King. His Majesty alighted, carrying a big bunch of roses which he presented to me, profoundly apologizing for the fact that they had got rather knocked about on the way. He told me they were special roses from the royal gardens and apologized again. I thought them beautiful and handed them to the caretaker with instructions to put them in water. The King was delighted with the castle, its splendid position and the well-kept park. He showed interest in everything, accepted an orangeade, was shown over the rooms and taken up to the top of the tower. On leaving he remarked that the place had none of the luxury befitting the home of a head of the government. To Benito he repeated his usual expressions of admiration and gratitude for his work and then left me with cordial thanks and kindly wishes for our future. He also said he had been gratified at the welcome he had received in the Romagna on his way to us, and that it was Mussolini he had to thank for it, as it was very different from the cold and unfriendly receptions he had previously met with.

From the top of the Rocca we all reviewed a procession of typical country carts, decked out in rustic finery and driven by peasants in costume. I do not know how they managed to stage all this, as the news of the King's visit had been announced very late, yet the organization was perfect. They brought their farm implements with them as well as the musical instruments from which they are never separated. Unfortunately they cheered far too much for the Duce, who had to keep pointing to the King to remind them that it was our guest they were supposed to be acclaiming.

His Majesty was in the best of spirits when he left us. I then looked for my roses, but found the good fellow to whom I had handed them tearing his hair because the flowers had been drowned in too much water and were now spoilt beyond recognition. Even the Savoy colours of the ribbon had run. I could not help being amused by the comic dismay of the caretaker.

Benito was very pleased with the way things had gone. He told me that he was thinking of having a small stone plaque put up to commemorate the event. It was I who dissuaded him. I felt instinctively that the King was not sincere.

CHAPTER XVIII

PEACE OR WAR?

CLOSE ON the heels of the *Anschluss* came the Sudeten question, which caused widespread panic because it was feared that we were on the verge of another world conflict.

Now, as then, I am asked the same question by many people: "Did Mussolini want war?" As the person most intimately and affectionately associated with him, particularly in the fearful years of Europe's ordeal, I am in the best position to answer that he did not. In fact, he dreaded it,

(Right) Mussolini with Sir Austen Chamberlain, the British Foreign Secretary, at Leghorn in 1926

(Below) Mussolini with Neville Chamberlain, the British Prime Minister, and Count Ciano, the Italian Foreign Minister, together in Rome early in 1939

Mussolini and Hitler at Munich at the time of the 1938 Crisis

Mussolini on a visit to Goering at his hunting lodge, Carinhall, near Berlin

because he foresaw "the damage which modern weapons would indubitably inflict on Italian territory, which is so exposed to air attack". I can say this in all sincerity, as I have already referred to his divided feelings in connection with the early stages of the Italo-German alliance, and to his ideas about the necessity for a European anti-bolshevik union and his intention to bring it about by peaceful means.

It is from this angle that the Munich Conference at the end of September 1938 must be approached. He believed it had definitely removed the threat of a second world war, whereas in fact it only secured a few months' respite.

Certain incidents about that time are not known to the general public. They are faithfully recorded in my diary:

"28th September, 1938. Benito did not even get back to lunch today. He spent the whole day at the Palazzo Venezia and arrived home, quite worn out, very late. I was anxiously waiting for him in the drawing-room, because rumours of war are spreading like wildfire. 'I don't know whether I shall be able to bring the Powers round to a peaceful and friendly discussion,' he said, with a frown, 'and can there be a conference in time? That's what I'm working for but they all seem bent on plunging to disaster, which might well mean the end of Europe.' 'Isn't there some other way out?' I asked, as I was frightened by these gloomy forebodings, coming from a natural optimist. 'Discussion, calm, dispassionate discussion, everyone laying aside national claims and ambitions and never losing sight of the common weal. It could even result in a confederation, a sort of United States of Europe.' The meeting was finally fixed up after a series of dramatic telephone conversations. He afterwards rang me up from the Palazzo Venezia. He was wildly excited. 'I've succeeded, Rachele! I've managed to arrange a meeting between Hitler, Chamberlain and Daladier. There's still hope. It's no small thing even to get the factions on to the same train.' "

He left in a hurry and telephoned from Munich with the curt remark: "The danger is averted. There will be no war."

I will not dwell on the spontaneous and enthusiastic demonstrations with which he was greeted on his return from Munich. I quote from my diary:

"1st October, 1938. Benito back from Bavaria, tired but happy. He is pleased with the demonstration he got in Rome. He came home at once and gave me some additional information: 'The outcome has exceeded my expectations. Chamberlain was very suspicious when he arrived. He was dubious about the upshot of the negotiations and it took me a long time to convince him that we were friendly. As for Hitler, his pride at having induced the representatives of France and England to wait on his decisions was plain to see. Daladier was the most amenable to persuasion. It is clear that France is not quite ready for a war. When Daladier saw the scales tilting towards a peaceful solution he seemed a changed man, so great was his pleasure. I interpreted for all three, as Hitler knows nothing but German, Chamberlain English and French, and Daladier only a little Italian. This made for better understanding.' "

I asked Benito a lot of questions about the part he played, but he was not forthcoming.

So ended that summer, for me the last summer of comparative peace and quiet. During the previous months I had left Italy for the first time for a tour through Tripolitania, but before that, I and Anna Maria, Romano, Orsola (my daughter-in-law) and Silvia (Vito's wife), had gone for a cruise on *Aurora*, Benito's private yacht. We had called at Zara, Lussino, Pola, Trieste and Venice. It was an entirely private affair and we were travelling at our own expense, yet we were given many an entirely unexpected welcome.

I was deeply touched at our departure from Zara. As the *Aurora* drew away, we witnessed the incredible spectacle of thousands of persons, who had come to see us off, kneeling on the quayside and remaining in that position till we were out of sight. At Brioni, Prince Aimone d'Aosta, Duke of Spoleto, came on board the yacht to greet us, profusely apologizing for having eaten garlic and explaining that he was very fond of it. When we went to Tripoli, also on *Aurora*, Orsola and her mother came with us. Vittorio accompanied us on the outward trip and returned by plane. At Tripoli we found Bruno, just back from shooting parties in Ethiopia. Official receptions were barred. I visited the new Italian settlements, and was warmly received throughout. I was surprised at what I considered the haughty and pompous attitude of Governor Italo Balbo. But I liked Tripolitania very much indeed; the fertility of its soil and the vast opportunities for colonization made me long to settle down there myself some day.

Chamberlain and Halifax came to Rome at the beginning of January 1939. Mussolini told me that this was the first result of his efforts at Munich to bring about "a peaceful revision of the treaties". The British Premier took an interest in everything, and his expressions of admiration for the Eternal City and Mussolini's policy were, according to Benito, "very sprightly for an Englishman". At the conclusion of the talks Chamberlain presented an autographed photograph of himself to Benito. It went to swell the collection of hundreds of such photographs which Mussolini received from prominent personages the world over. We used to keep the photographs in a small drawing-room at the Rocca delle Camminate.

Benito went on to tell me about the results: "I'm not dissatisfied. It is as well to keep relations with Great Britain on a friendly footing, even if, in certain spheres, our interests obviously conflict." With a shy smile he added, "the reception they got was impressive, but the Romans showed no particular warmth or enthusiasm. Evidently they have not forgotten sanctions. I believe Chamberlain noticed it. Both he and Lord Halifax were friendly, however, and proved receptive and accommodating."

Before the British Premier's arrival Mussolini jokingly warned me that "Chamberlain and his umbrella" were coming. During their stay in Rome, every time he telephoned or came home to tell me what was going on he always used the formula: "Chamberlain and the umbrella." On the day of the reception at the Capitol, Mussolini telephoned me from the Palazzo Venezia and said, in a serious tone of voice, "Rachele, it's happened at last. Chamberlain has lost his umbrella! Someone's taken it from the Capitol, and the police are exceedingly worried." A few hours later he rang up again and said with a laugh, "I know you're worrying about Chamberlain's umbrella. We've found it. No one had taken it. It had got mixed up with other umbrellas which have turned up in his honour at the Capitol."

A month later the Catholic world, and Italy its centre, suffered a great loss. Pope Pius XI died. Benito deeply mourned his passing. "Christianity has lost a great Pope. We have lost the Pope of the Conciliation."

It was Pope Ratti himself who coined the expression "Man of Providence", for Mussolino. (I might mention in this connection that the last sister of Pius X, Pope Sarto, left my husband a skull-cap and an ornamental platter which had belonged to her brother. During the Social republic, on Mussolini's instructions, these gifts were delivered for safe keeping to Cardinal Schuster.)

There were various rumours spread in high circles in Rome—
rumours reported both in the national and foreign press, to
the effect that Mussolini had influenced the election of Cardinal
Eugenio Pacelli. This was fantastic. I quote Mussolini's words
to me on that occasion:

"Neither I nor the Italian government have ever interfered,
nor do we intend to interfere, in the Vatican's religious policy.
The election of Cardinal Pacelli is the Sacred College's business.
We like him because he co-operated in the Lateran pacts."
And my husband was very grateful for the words uttered by
the new Pontiff during an audience granted to newly-wedded
couples in June 1939: "On him in whose hands lie the destinies
of our country may the Lord bestow his favour and abundant
blessing."

With peace not yet a lost cause, two outstanding events in
March and April were highly advantageous to the régime:
the end of the Spanish war with the capture of Barcelona and
Madrid and Franco's victory, and the occupation of Albania.

The Albanian enterprise (7th–9th April, 1939) was very
dear to the heart of our son-in-law, Galeazzo Ciano, then
Minister for Foreign Affairs, and rigorously advocated by him.
Mussolini, though dubious at first, was ultimately won over,
partly as the result of what he described as "the shifty attitude
of King Zog, who takes Italian money while flirting with
Belgrade and Moscow". He often told me that he had "cau-
tioned" the Albanian King, of whom he wished to make (to
use his exact words) "a sincere and reliable ally, so that
Albania may become an anti-bolshevik bulwark across the
Adriatic". Yet the credit for the success of the undertaking
went to Galeazzo Ciano, whom the King rewarded with the
Collar of the Annunziata, a decoration he greatly coveted and
for which he was always pressing.

Early in May 1939, Galeazzo, who at that time was playing
a leading part in international affairs, concluded with von
Ribbentrop the "Pact of Steel", which had had its first begin-
nings during Benito's first visit to Germany. Mussolini had this
to say about the pact and the diplomatic meetings then in
full swing between Germany and Italy on the one side and
Hungary, Yugoslavia and Rumania on the other:

"The west must be organized as one unit and we must set
up our own western system to oppose the eastern one. The
Pact of Steel front will also help to counterbalance England's
predominance in Europe, but this does not mean that we are

seeking isolation. Proof to the contrary is the 'Gentlemen's Agreement' which partly stems from the old Stresa agreements."

The Steel Pact business was almost immediately followed by the sudden death of Admiral Costanzo Ciano, Galeazzo's father. It was a hard blow for Benito, who immediately left for the Admiral's home at Ponte a Moriano and arrived on the morning of his death (27th June, 1939). There the Duce met the King Emperor, who had been equally prompt. My husband was greatly moved and anxious to pay a last tribute in the form of the Roman salute to the departed. I and Benito attended the funeral which took place the following morning and was extremely impressive. I read in my diary:

"We have lost one of the few people to whom my husband confided the greatest secrets. Duke Amedeo of Aosta was at my side at the funeral for some time, talking most respectfully of the deceased. He reminded me of an episode which occurred at the time of the March on Rome: 'Signora,' he said, 'we have Mussolini to thank for the fact that the House of Savoy is still reigning in Italy and I admire him immensely for what he has done for our country. I may say that I have been one of his followers since the March on Rome; when the Fascists were marching past the Quirinal, I was in the Piazza wearing a black shirt. I entered the Palace by a service entrance hiding the shirt so as to escape the King's displeasure.' While he was speaking, Duke Aimone of Spoleto had joined us and was nodding his head in assent."

CHAPTER XIX

WAR BEGINS

THE SUMMER of 1939 marked the outbreak of the tragic, long-dreaded, world conflict. Diplomatic contacts between Rome and Berlin had become ever closer after the conclusion of the Pact of Steel. Mussolini, who had entered into the alliance in the hope of inducing Hitler to take a more pacific line, grew increasingly anxious as he realized that the German leader meant to force the pace.

The concern with which Benito viewed the fast approaching conflict was two-fold. In the first place—to quote his words: "You know how a war begins but never how it may end; wars have only deferred, never finally decided, the quarrels of nations." Secondly, because (also in his own words): "Italy's military preparations are inadequate for another war." He told me over and over again that "the conquest of Ethiopia and the Spanish conflict drained our stocks of raw materials, of which there is almost a chronic shortage."

For some time, Bruno, whose service in the Air Force gave him plenty of opportunity to form a judgment of men and their achievements, had been enlightening me about a certain amount of confusion prevailing in the directives issued in quarters responsible for military preparations. He spoke of certain officers who were mainly concerned with keeping in the official eye, promoting their careers and claiming that they did more than their duty, while some of the generals were only too ready with the standard phrase, "Duce, we await your orders, we are ready," to conceal a very different state of affairs.

I can truthfully say that I myself tried to help my husband to pierce the smoke-screen and see the reality behind. I could quote very many examples, but a few must suffice.

One day the Under-Secretary for Air came to the Rocca delle Camminate for the purpose of visiting the Caproni aircraft factory which had been built near Predappio. The Under-Secretary went round, promised to supply the equipment for hundreds of planes. Some time later it was announced that hundreds of these new types had already been equipped. Actually, the material which reached Predappio was only enough to equip two—I mean two—planes. Inquiries made as a result of my exposures invariably showed that my statements had been absolutely correct. Faced with the facts, the angry Benito used to say, "Ninety-nine times out of a hundred, Mother is right."

Realizing that a climax was approaching, he instructed Attolico, the Italian Ambassador to Germany, to warn Berlin of the exact position of our armaments. It was while pondering this move that one evening at the Villa Torlonia he confidentially remarked, "I only hope my bluntness succeeds in curbing the Fuehrer's impetuosity." But there was to be no repetition of the miracle of Munich.

I can honestly say that, in my husband's view, the Non-Aggression Pact" between Germany and Russia gave the *coup de grâce* to peace.

Mussolini was very surprised, not by the pact itself (he had always urged Hitler to seek a *modus vivendi* with Russia as part of a peaceful co-existence policy between Western Europe and the Soviet Union) but because, as he told me, he clearly saw "that the pact is nothing but a pretext for war".

After this unexpected event diplomatic activity between the various European capitals was intensified, particularly in the direction of Rome, to which all the powers looked to pull off another Munich.

Every day—and sometimes twice a day—Mussolini and Ciano received the ambassadors to the Quirinal, especially those of Germany, France and Great Britain. I remember how, on one single day, 25th August, Ambassador Von Mackensen brought three messages from Hitler. Benito replied to the third from the Villa Torlonia at ten o'clock in the evening. When I referred to the nervous strain imposed on him he simply answered, "It's necessary, Rachele. It's necessary because of the vast issues at stake . . . perhaps the future of European, or indeed of world, civilization."

One evening, at the end of August, Benito announced the grave news to me, "It's war. No agreement could be reached, because both sides are set on a show-down." I was dumbfounded and at once asked whether it would be possible to limit the conflict. "I don't know," he replied. "Wars are like landslides, you can't forsee their duration or direction. There have been wars lasting a hundred years." Then he noticed my downcast looks and assumed a jocular tone to cheer me up: "But I shall do everything possible to restrict the war to a German–Polish clash."

Germany launched her ultimatum to Poland on 31st August and then marched in. From that day on, there was no room in Benito's thoughts for anything except Italy's destiny. He once said, "It's now impossible to keep out of the war and even more impossible, and dangerous, not to enter it on Germany's side. The Russo–German pact makes Germany unbeatable by any other Power or coalition."

He nevertheless invented the concept of non-belligerence, which he defined at supper one evening as "almost a miracle of balancing which will give us a chance of living in precarious peace for a few months, perhaps more, on the brink of the conflagration. I still hope that non-belligerence may enable me to bring the warring nations together on the lines of the Four Power Pact."

History has on record his efforts at the conclusion of the Polish campaign, and Hitler's favourable response which was rejected by Britain.

Mussolini's fear of a German invasion of Italy increased with every move of her armies. I have more than once heard him say, as if arguing the case with himself: "England cannot stand up against the German war machine. The United States is too far off and even if the Americans decide to come in they will not be able to build up a war effort sufficient to turn the tide before Germany's final victory. If we do not make common cause with Germany, Italy may find herself occupied in a matter of months, if not days."

Sumner Welles, Roosevelt's special envoy, came to Rome on 25th February, 1940, and had a long interview with Mussolini the following day. Benito afterwards told me he had been very frank with him in setting out Italy's position, emphasising the Italian claims which must be satisfied and his own determination to do everything possible to prolong Italian "non-belligerence" and circumscribe the conflict. "He seems to be a modern Colonel House," Benito added, "and this time too it looks as if the mission is doomed to failure for the very same reasons."

The German government was evidently concerned over Sumner Welles's visit to Rome and on 9th March, the day after the envoy's visit to Berlin, Hitler sent Foreign Minister Von Ribbentrop to Rome to use powerful arguments to overcome any objections we might have to an extension of the war. Even at that stage Von Ribbentrop clearly betrayed, though in the most diplomatic terms, Germany's intention to occupy Italy in a military sense if we let them down over the Pact of Steel.

The German armies went from victory to victory and each new success increased the clamour from King Victor Emmanuel, many generals and party leaders and the general public for Italy's entry into the war.

On the 30th May Mussolini's inner torment reached a crisis when President Roosevelt sent him a personal message pleading with him to keep out of the fray. I remember how he brought home a pile of photographs and several films of German military operations. We had the films shown on the screen at the Villa Torlonia and I still recall how incredibly impressive they were. The German armies seemed a hurricane sweeping every obstacle aside and overwhelming all resistance.

"What a formidable show of military power," Benito exclaimed, "and now they're on our doorstep. Whether we come
in or stay out, the Germans will occupy the whole of Europe,
and if we don't make a contribution in blood they alone will
dictate the pattern of Europe's future existence. Their terms
will mean the elimination of Latin civilization. Everyone's
clamouring for war now; even the few who opposed the Pact
of Steel have changed their minds and many are saying what a
poor figure we shall cut by coming in last."

It was against that background that Italy entered the war.

CHAPTER XX

FIRST VICTORIES—FIRST BEREAVEMENTS

OUR SONS Bruno and Vittorio, posted to Grottaglia airport
as pilots, were among the first to leave, while Edda joined up
as a Red Cross nurse. Many ministers, party leaders and
personalities, also donned the grey-green uniforms, often only
for a few months, as if the whole thing were a sort of holiday,
or pleasant break in which to collect medals and commissions.

The first month of war brought the armistice with France
and the tragic death of Italo Balbo.

Hitler and Mussolini did not see eye to eye over the Italo-
German armistice with France. Benito urged military occupation of the French colonies in Africa "for purely strategic
reasons for the duration of the war". Hitler disagreed because,
"he was certain of victory by now," to use my husband's own
words.

I also remember the words in which Benito gave vent to
his annoyance: "Hitler wants to play the magnanimous. I
was keener than he on leaving France with a French government, but the French colonies constitute a danger until final
victory has been achieved. Hitler has made a grave strategic
blunder. Let's hope that his optimism about future developments will prove my fears are unfounded."

Italo Balbo's dramatic end shocked and greatly grieved
my husband. Of the Quadrumvir he had this to say: "Balbo
had some faults, like any other man. But he did great work
in Libya. We shall miss him."

From the very start of Italian military operations the sad, bad habit of pretending that everything was going well took firm hold of many of Benito's colleagues, and the few who dared speak the truth were kept in the background and even ostracized. I had often tried to put my husband wise to the practice, which in the long run only harmed the country, and I redoubled my efforts. In vain, however, because he was apt to consider it unthinkable that any associate of his could intentionally shirk duty and let him down. But there were plenty of examples of inefficiency, and it was these that upset Mussolini most. He particularly, and often, deplored the indolence and lack of drive of the Crown Prince, who commanded the armies on the Western Front. I myself disliked the all too-frequent communiqués eulogizing the more or less heroic exploits of high party leaders, and duly protested to the appropriate Ministry of Popular Culture.

At the end of 1940 the Russo–Finnish war broke out. It is well known that the heroic resistance of the Finns was universally admired, but what is not well known is that that war sowed the seeds of the Axis defeat. It was the Russian army's apparent inability to fight a modern war that fired Hitler with the idea of a rapid conquest of that country. But it is only fair to say that Mussolini took a very different view. He believed that Russia's attack on Finland was a pitfall for the unwary. Russia could have swallowed Finland in a matter of days, if Stalin had really wanted. Mussolini conveyed his views to Hitler in a letter sent through the Italian Ambassador in Berlin, as he already suspected that the Fuehrer, now gloating over the weaknesses of the Red armies, was beginning to think of revising the Russo–German Non-Aggression Pact.

As I have said before, it is not my task to record in detail the political and diplomatic events of the war. I only refer to them insofar as they affected our home life. Of course the ever growing anxieties over the course of the campaigns in North Africa, Ethiopia and Albania, and things like the severe aerial bombardments of the principal Italian towns, touched us very closely. In March 1941, while Benito was visiting the front during the campaign in Greece, we had a nasty shock. I will quote from my diary:

"I woke up suddenly after a crazy dream. I was describing it to Ernestina, my maid, when I was called to the telephone. Filled with forebodings, I picked up the receiver. Benito's voice came through clear but very excited, 'Listen, Edda has fallen into the sea.' (I have already said that my husband could never bring himself to use a bit of tact when breaking bad news. He was gruff, embarrassed and no good at all on such occasions. Meeting Prince Torlonia one day, when the latter was suffering from a large boil, Benito could find nothing more consoling to say than, 'I once had a friend with the same trouble and he died almost at once.') 'She was in the water for five hours, but she's all right now,' Benito continued. 'I'm flying over to see her.' 'But how did it happen?' I asked. 'I'll tell you all about it when I get back. See you soon.' We were then cut off. I rang up the Air and Navy ministries, but at first hand they knew no more than what my husband had told them. I find that putting all this down relieves my anxiety a bit."

The next day's entry runs:

"Benito has sent me a long cable from army headquarters in Albania describing Edda's dramatic adventure. 'The hospital ship *Po* was hit at night by seven English bombs and quickly sank. Edda was still awake in her cabin when the planes came over. She instinctively snatched up a coat, rushed out and knocked at the door of a close friend of hers, also a Red Cross nurse, who had studied with her at Milan. The blast from the bomb had caused the cabin door to stick, and the poor girl inside was calling for help. Meanwhile the ship was slowly heeling over, the water was rising and Edda felt half paralysed with horror. Eventually a sailor ran past her and pushed her into the sea. She managed to keep afloat in the pitch darkness for five hours, numb with cold, but trying to help people around her. Rescue operations only started at dawn. Now she has recovered and is quite well.' "

A few days later I recorded:

"The Duce flew back from Albania yesterday and came home. One glance at his face was sufficient to show me that things were going badly. 'That front is cursed!' he exclaimed. 'The troops are doing their best, and this time supplies are getting up all right, yet we're not able to break through.' He went on to tell me about the enthusiastic reception he got from the soldiers. But from the very outset he had not liked the plans for the offensive and had said as much to the generals, who nevertheless continued to be optimistic. After the first phases of the battle, he remarked to Cavallero, 'But this is a failure!'

"He also told me of a strange incident. While the car was

threading its way towards an observation post considered suitable for following the course of the action, he distinctly heard someone say in Romagna dialect, 'Don't go up there, Duce; don't go, they mean to kill you! I'm talking in dialect so they won't understand.' Benito paid no heed to the warning (fanaticism has often been responsible for some crazy ideas among his entourage) but it was nice to hear the Romagna dialect in those remote mountains and he leaned out of the car to see who had spoken. All he could make out was a private soldier being overpowered and bundled off by some others. He could not tell the driver to stop, because this would have blocked the traffic. He reached the observation post, watched the attack, and withdrew a quarter of an hour ahead of time. A few minutes afterwards the post was hit by a shell and a splinter was embedded in the telescope, mounted on a tripod, by which the Duce had been standing for some considerable time.

"While telling me all this, Benito handed me the telescope still complete with the splinter. He was keeping it as a souvenir. 'Could the Romagnolo have been right? Where is the front now? Will they have another try?' I said. But I realized what he was going through and did not press for an answer. He had much to say about his visit to Edda, who will soon be home on convalescent leave."

The war in Greece ended a few weeks later, as a result of a converging movement by Italian and German troops. Yugoslavia's surrender brought us a new ally, Croatia, though it was to prove a hot-bed of trouble for our soldiers.

While the Balkan situation had been satisfactorily cleared up for the time being, our army was still in retreat in North Africa.

After the end of the war in Greece Bruno was transferred to Pisa, where he was posted to the long-range, four-engined bomber group, and prior to the equipment of the aircraft with some new instruments he spent a month in Germany, where he had been invited to visit the buildings and airfields destined for Atlantic flights. On his return to Italy he gave his father a political survey. He was filled with admiration for the sense of discipline of the German people, who were not wilting under the burden of this hardest of wars. "The German people," he once remarked to me, "may lose the war, but Germany will always be a top-rank nation."

When he got back to Rome in June 1941 his contacts with

ministerial circles gave him great cause for concern. He told me bluntly that the bureaucratic machine was moving in one direction only—towards defeat. "Father has an enormous lot to do," he added, "but the worst thing is the amount of sabotage going on." On 30th July he came to say good-bye. He was more expansive than usual. Suddenly he asked me to look after his wife and the little Marina. "If anything should happen, you must keep them with you always." He seemed rather upset, and I have often thought of his words since. Next morning he kissed me good-bye when he was leaving for Pisa. I told him to be careful and not forget to write. "There are times when it's no use being careful," he gravely answered.

I often see him as he looked that morning, framed in the doorway of my room, tall and strong, with the face of a boy who has grown up too fast.

CHAPTER XXI

WAR IN THE EAST—BRUNO'S DEATH

It was the last time I saw him alive.

Tragedy descended on our family like a thunderbolt. I had not the heart to put anything in my diary when the news of Bruno's death came. Benito subsequently filled the gap with his book *Parlo con Bruno* (I Talk to Bruno).

Now I can only rely on my memories, and even after so many eventful years they are as vivid as on that terrible day. I re-live the nightmare: my distraught husband's words on the telephone, my consternation, the endless flight to Pisa in a storm, my grim endurance—it was not even courage—till I saw Bruno again.

He was lying on a cot, swathed in bandages, except for his face which still had the calm, untroubled look of a child. Gina, his wife, had been in Pisa before the disaster. The family gathered round him, and the sight of Benito, suffering in silence, cut me to the quick. It is only in recent times that the vision of that horror has to some extent faded, thanks to the thought that Bruno died with the vision of an Italy still set on victory and the knowledge that he had not disgraced his uniform.

The inquiry that followed was very thorough, but I considered there was no point in it. What point was there in establishing that at 7.45 a.m. on 7th August, 1941, Bruno had reported at the airfield and taken off at 8.5 a.m., and that survivors said that though all the engines had suddenly cut out Bruno had shown great presence of mind and done his best to prevent disaster, keeping his aircraft under control till the very last moment. Also that his last words were, "Dad . . . the field!"

Somebody even mentioned the possibility of sabotage.

I shall always remember the crowds that gathered at Pisa, Florence, Forlì and Predappio to pay a last tribute to my son. The body was placed in a sarcophagus of stone quarried from near the Rocca and buried in the little cemetery of San Cassiano. The only inscription was the dates of birth and death. Many times since has the little chapel been smothered in flowers and a votive lamp presented by the mothers of Lucca airmen is always kept burning there. On 7th August, 1945, some British R.A.F. officers paid their respects to the grave of the gallant pilot who was my son, and covered it with flowers.

Bruno's death was harder for Benito to bear because he could not give rein to his feelings but must carry on with his work, which was becoming ever more burdensome. I alone am in a position to know what strength of mind he needed to bear up against the blow. In the pages of *Parlo con Bruno* he lays bare his soul and betrays the resigned melancholy which from that moment began to possess him.

We did not know it but we still had ahead of us the saddest pages in the story of the war, including certain inexplicable incidents—tankers which reached their destination safely only to blow up just as they entered harbour and systematic sabotage of arms and equipment. Nor had I yet heard what returned prisoners of war and soldiers on leave from Africa had to tell me about drums of petrol mixed with water. All this was the result of disloyalty, corruption and the frustrated, disappointed ambitions of mediocrities who were contributing to their country's ruin.

With a view to reducing Benito's anxieties, I once, and only once, approached Bocchini, the Chief of Police, and asked him to look into the true character of a then very prominent party leader. After an inquiry lasting three months, Benito fully confirmed my suspicions.

It was just because Mussolini's strong views on Russia's potential capabilities were well known in Berlin that Hitler did not inform him of the German preparations for war against the bolsheviks. One night in June 1941 the telephone at my bedside roused me from sleep. What could anyone want at that time of night? It was the German military attaché in Rome, who urgently wanted to speak to the Duce. When I asked him whether he could not ring up later, so that I need not wake up my husband, the attaché would not be put off and eventually blurted out the reason for precipitancy, "It is my duty to tell you of Germany's declaration of war on Russia." I rushed into Benito's room and woke him. He came to the telephone and, not confining himself to listening in, had a long and heated discussion in German. Furiously angry, he then turned to me, "They're mad! It means ruin to us! I don't believe Russia would ever have attacked us. Germany knows how to make war but nothing about politics."

He did not go back to bed but left immediately for Rome. Shortly afterwards he decided to send an Italian expeditionary force to the new front, under the command of General Messe, giving as his reason, "We must contribute all we can to secure a 'blitz' victory. If Russia is not defeated in the first few months, she will never be defeated at all."

Our daughter Edda, who had recovered from her misadventure in the waters off Albania, volunteered for service on the Russian front. She spent three months at Stalino, just behind the front line. I have something to say about the Russian operations in my diary:

"4th August, 1941. Benito came home quite pleased and showed me a telegram from General Messe. Our soldiers are continuing their advance, overcoming Russian resistance. 'You see how necessary it was to show our flag there too,' he said. 'We must show the world that it isn't only the Germans who can win battles.'

"7th October, 1941. Hitler personally informed Mussolini of the taking of Orel. 'Orel is the gateway to Moscow,' Benito told me. 'But they must close the net quickly as winter is not far away.'"

The Duce knew the peculiarities of the Russian front and its particular strategic problems as he, Vittorio and Hitler had flown over in the same plane to visit the Italian Expeditionary Force in the Ukraine. It was mid-summer, and they had travelled for hours over a seemingly unending corn-

growing area. On his return, Benito had a good deal to say
about those vast areas which produce essential food in such
abundance. He deplored the fact that "the Germans are so
harsh to the civil population in the occupied territories and
are trying to maintain themselves by stripping the country,
forgetting that the victor should treat the vanquished
humanely".

The autumn did not bring the expected decision on the
Russian front, and with the outbreak of war between Japan
and the United States in the winter the Triple Alliance found
itself up against nearly all the republics of North and South
America. I remember Mussolini's anger against Roosevelt, of
whom he always had a very poor opinion. "He's a meddler
whose actions have always been calculated to lead to war.
His physical paralysis is the secret origin of his political outlook." For Churchill, however, tough and implacable enemy
though he was, he had a high regard. "He's a real John Bull,"
he used to say, "a staunch friend and a stubborn foe, one of
the great Europeans of our time who realizes Europe's future
needs even though, as an Englishman, he cannot help to
provide for them."

Russia's winter offensive, aided by exceptionally severe
weather, dispelled all hopes of an early end to the war on the
eastern front. Benito anxiously followed the reports about the
new position on the Italian sector and grumbled that the
Germans had not kept their promises to provide our forces
with arms and equipment suitable for operations in such a
climate and such difficult country, as a result of which our
men had to fight under conditions of shocking inferiority. The
bad news coming in from the Russian front coincided with
the second withdrawal in Libya where, however, the situation
was soon restored by the capture of Tobruk and the advance to
El Alamein.

People will hardly credit the stringent orders Mussolini
gave at the beginning of the war to ensure that the family
standard of living conformed to the general regulations for
the reduction of consumption, and what pains he took to
see that his orders were obeyed. We gave up our usual Sunday
drives. Benito himself only used a car for official journeys
between the Villa Torlonia and the Palazzo Venezia. I gave
up my car altogether. The children walked to school, despite
Anna Maria's poor health. To save rubber, we turned down
a friend's offer to take Anna Maria to school in an electric

car. In those days I used to take food almost daily to a home for the children of civil prisoners at Monte Mario. I used to go by bus until one of the nuns in the home mentioned the matter to Cardinal Pizzardo and he placed his private car at my disposal.

On 11th March, 1942, there was a Requiem Mass in the Church of the Sudario for the Duke of Aosta, Viceroy of Ethiopia, who was captured by the British and died in a Nairobi clinic. The service was attended by their Majesties and the highest in the land, including many holders of the Collare dell'Annunziata. I went by bus, with my daughter-in-law Gina. When the service was over, the congregation gathered at the church door to watch the departure of their Majesties. After the latter had left, I noticed that no one else moved and an usher was trying to locate my car. My husband's rank gave me precedence after their Majesties. Galeazzo Ciano, who was present, asked me why I had not come by car and offered me his own, but I showed him the bus ticket I had on me, refused his offer and left as I had come.

The situation of the Axis and Japanese forces at the beginning of summer 1942 was most satisfactory, with great strategic operations developing successfully. In Russia, where our Expeditionary Force had been expanded and was now called ARM.I.R. under the command of General Gariboldi, the Don was reached and spearheads got as far as the Caucasus. In North Africa, General Rommel, who had been promoted to the rank of marshal, was preparing a drive on Alexandria from the El Alamein front. This was the high-water mark, when the Italo-German forces seemed to have victory in their grasp. But it was also the end of our successes, and was followed by a series of setbacks and retreats.

Benito left for the African front on 29th June and did not get back till the evening of 21st July. My diary runs:

"I welcomed my husband home this evening, after his long absence. He is tanned by the African sun though, unlike previous occasions, it has not done him any good. He is thinner and definitely looks tired. 'What's the matter with you?' I asked. He hesitated for an instant: 'Nothing. Just a bit of stomach trouble, but I'll get over it. It's the war that's not going well.' As if to avoid further questioning, he took me into his study to tell me about his doings in Africa. Having called in at Athens on his way back, he talked about the situation in Greece which he described as 'unsatisfactory, because

8

the Germans are, as usual, too harsh, and there's a food shortage.' He immediately gave orders for the despatch of food supplies and other relief."

CHAPTER XXII

BENITO'S ILLNESS

THE COURSE of the war had a direct influence on Mussolini's health, and in fact it was at the crucial moments, when the fate of the Italian army was at stake, that his physical condition was affected most. The early stages of the disasters in Libya coincided with a return of his old stomach trouble. I will quote from my diary at that time:

"2nd July, 1942. Benito complaining of his old pains and, without saying anything to him, I have started plain cooking. It is obvious that he also needs a rest and I made no bones about it at dinner tonight. I did not get the usual reaction, so I am certain that he has completely worn himself out in Africa.

"10th September, 1942. I had a long talk with Professor Castellani. I told him I knew how devoted he was to the Duce and so he must tell me the whole truth about Mussolini's continuous loss of weight which is worrying me a lot. Castellani reassured me, insisting that the trouble is simply dysentery which he thinks the Duce must have contracted in Libya during a spell of great heat. It is a tiresome disease, but can be effectively cured. But how can you be expected to remain calm and collected when your husband is in such pain and when the developments at the front are continually adding to his worries?

"13th September, 1942. I have been badgering Castellani again, and today he suggested we might call in Professor Frugoni for a consultation. It is not the first time Frugoni's name has been mentioned in our house. Castellani, like the perfect gentleman he is, has no feeling of professional jealousy with regard to other doctors.

"16th September, 1942. I hesitated for various reasons but have yielded to family pressure and decided to call in Frugoni. We shall see what he says. Meanwhile Benito goes on losing weight. I cannot help having uncomfortable suspicions about that wretched tour in Libya.

"28th September, 1942. Frugoni has been here and examined Mussolini thoroughly. He said that Castellani has 'a bee in his bonnet about dysentery' and thinks himself it is most likely a return of the old ulcer trouble.

"3rd November, 1942. As Frugoni cannot attend Mussolini regularly, he has appointed his assistant, Dr. Arnaldo Pozzi, to look after him. If only there was better news from the front my husband would recover his spirits too, but unfortunately the British have been attacking in Egypt for the last ten days and our troops are retreating.

"9th November, 1942. This is certainly a month of bad news. The landing of the Americans in Algeria has helped to make Benito's general condition worse. Now Dr. Pozzi is coming almost every day to give him intravenous injections, but so far I do not see any improvement and Benito is still losing weight.

"15th November, 1942. Our troops have occupied Nice and landed in Corsica. The Duce showed no pleasure whatever in giving me the news as our retreat in Libya has not ended. Dr. Pozzi is continuing to give him intravenous injections.

"25th November, 1942. I have succeeded in making Benito take things quietly and stop the beastly injections which have often upset him and cause swelling of the veins. To the misfortunes in Libya is now added the continuous bombing of the big cities in the north and the Duce tires himself out with long telephone conversations with the Prefects of the stricken cities; he is always particularly anxious to know whether the rescue and relief teams have arrived promptly.

"30th November, 1942. Tonight the Duce had a long talk with Goering, who has arrived unexpectedly in Rome. It would seem that there have been serious differences between Rommel and Bastico. Goering has promised men and material.

"2nd December, 1942. Yesterday the Duce insisted on going out, although it cannot be said that he has recovered. Today he spoke in the Chamber. I am not in the habit of attending the sittings, but this time I should have liked to turn up and see the faces of the many who swear by my husband but are not ashamed to be glad when they hear the news of his illness. However, all things considered, I thought it better to stay at home, as if I had met any of these gentry I would have told them what I thought of them. I am told that it was those false friends who cheered the Duce's speech loudest.

"12th December, 1942. Dr. Frugoni is attending my husband again. I spoke to him myself, as I have heard that Benito will be going to Germany very soon, and I do not think that this is a good time in view of his health, although he shows signs of improvement. The strain of a long journey would undo what little good has been done.

"16th December, 1942. The Duce is not going to Germany. He has sent Ciano, who is young and will not be any the worse for a two days' train journey. While reading me some reports from Berlin containing bad news of the war in Russia, Benito burst out, 'Why on earth did the Fuehrer stick his head in that hornet's nest? What's he waiting for before trying to come to terms?

"25th December, 1942. Sad Christmas: in Libya and Russia there's not a sign of improvement and Benito has had to take to his bed again.

"9th January, 1943. I am writing these notes at Rocca delle Camminate. I have tried all I can to get the doctors to stop their treatments, but without success. Any child can see that things are not going well. I have never seen Benito suffering like this before. He can hardly get out of bed and when he managed to do so for a visit to the Palazzo Venezia, it was by sheer will power. I got so infuriated that, in desperation, I decided to leave. I want the doctors to face up fairly and squarely to their responsibilities for their treatment, with which I do not agree. Irma is to ring me up every two hours.

"10th January, 1943. I had a sudden telephone call from Rome today. It was my husband. The weary tones of his voice upset me very much: 'Rachele, I am still ill,' he said. 'I've decided to join you and see if I can get better at Rocca.' The news that he will soon be here has given me fresh hope. The idea that I shall be able to look after him here, in our own house, in peace and quiet, fills me with joy.

"12th January, 1943. Benito is with me at last. As soon as he entered the Rocca he smiled with relief. He has brought Dr. Pozzi with him. Let us hope that the air of Romagna will perform the miracle the doctors have not been able to bring off.

"14th January, 1943. The Duce is extremely worried about the fate of Tripoli and this naturally aggravates the pains in his stomach. Can it be that nothing can be done for this illness? I have had a long conversation with Dr. Pozzi and have told him how distressed I am. He himself is not at all easy in his mind; he is particularly concerned about the very severe pains Benito had this morning. What worries me most of all is a letter which Professor Frugoni has sent me through his private secretary, De Cesare; a terrible letter (which he asks me to destroy after reading) in which he writes that he thinks that Mussolini has cancer at an advanced stage, and his life is in danger. I do not believe it at all and am keeping the information to myself. I am relieved to know that Benito has agreed to another consultation with Professor Frugoni and Professor Cesa Bianchi. I suggested the latter myself, as he might almost be called the old family doctor; he got Sandrino well and attended the Duce himself in 1925. Dr. Pozzi will fix up the consultation.

"17th January, 1943. A bit of relief at last. The consultation took place today and as soon as Professors Cesa Bianchi and Frugoni entered Benito's room, it was clear that there was a current of mutual confidence between doctors and patient. The examination was long and extremely thorough. Cancer was not mentioned at all. Eventually Cesa Bianchi assured the Duce that there was nothing serious, apart from a stubborn inflammation. He stayed on a bit for a general talk with Benito and I must admit that I had my heart in my mouth because I thought it might be the usual game of hiding the truth from the patient. I was wrong. When we left the room and I insisted on him telling me everything Cesa Bianchi looked at me with surprise, 'But I've already said there is absolutely nothing. He is very run down, that's all. Even the old ulcer is completely cured.' I mentioned the possibility of cancer and got a categorical answer, 'No signs whatever of cancer.' Whatever the reason, my husband has felt better today; he got up and came down to dinner.

"22nd January, 1943. Here we are back in Rome. It seems to me that the critical stage in the Duce's illness is behind us; his appetite has improved and he looks better.

"23rd January, 1943. Today the country has been informed of the loss of Tripoli. What dismay it has created. The Duce, sore at heart, told me the previous evening but I had not the courage to ask him for details. Now all our hopes are concentrated on the defence of Tunis.

"6th February, 1943. I am being pestered with telephone calls from people clamouring for information about the practically wholesale changes among the ministers which took place yesterday. Only last week we had a new chief for the army; Ambrosio has replaced Marshal Cavallero. Now Grandi, Buffarini, Pacolini, Bottai and others have been dismissed and it is likely that Ciano will be appointed Ambassador to the Holy See, at his own request. I am telling everyone that I know nothing about the reason for these changes. It is the first time that such indiscreet questions have been addressed to me but I realize that everyone is very worried about the general situation, and extremely anxious for news.

"The real truth of the matter is that Benito has for a long time been aware of intrigues against him amongst people he has dismissed (of course I cannot breathe a word of that to anyone). The ringleader is Cavallero who has been plotting to remove Mussolini and even kidnap me. I was supposed to disappear a few days before my husband's arrest! Mussolini's object in these ministerial changes is to placate the anger of a large section of the public with these men and meet their more specific criticism of Ciano.

"With the dismissal *en bloc* of Cavallero and these ministers, the Cavallero plot has been exposed, and Mussolini assures me that Cavallero is letting everyone know that he is truly contrite.

"20th February, 1943. We are back at the Rocca again. Benito's colour is coming back and he is putting on weight. I hope that a short rest in the country will do him a lot of good.

"25th February, 1943. In Rome. The situation is too serious and nothing I could say would induce my husband to prolong his stay in the Romagna. He is very upset about the bombing of Milan, Turin and Naples and spends hours on end on the telephone, even at night, personally instructing the Prefects and insisting on knowing whether everything possible has been done for the unfortunate people who have had their houses destroyed. He is lost in admiration for the patience and resolution of the Neapolitans under the continual air raids. 'We must reward them,' he said. When a ship loaded with ammunition blew up in that port, and the local authorities (the Prefect was away at the time) proved helpless, he was furious, rang up Rome and gave orders that the city should be kept in a state of continuous alert. 'So now we are down to treason and brazen sabotage!' he said to me. Of course his physical condition is affected by these great nervous shocks, but what can we do? I fully realize that in these dreadful moments Italy is the only thing that counts. I try to keep a sharp eye on my husband all day and every day and give him good food to stimulate his appetite.

"2nd March, 1943. Yesterday Professor Frugoni was here again. Benito has cut down on his meals again and I'm at my wits' end as the doctor says that he thinks the anæmia is getting worse owing to lack of nourishment. But there are no new developments. It looks as if there is some hope of holding out in Tunis. May it be true! I am sure that better news from the front would do my husband more good than any medicine.

"26th March, 1943. The Anglo-American offensive in Africa seems to have been checked after fluctuating fighting at Mareth. Benito himself gave me the news of this setback for the famous 8th Army, and also told me that he is contemplating another meeting with Hitler. So just as it looks as if his health is improving, he will have to face the strain of another journey to Germany. I have insisted that if the doctors do not approve of the journey, he must send someone else to see Hitler.

"30th March, 1943. Dr. Pozzi, after a few days' reflection, has told me that the Duce may go to Germany provided he travels by train.

"6th April, 1943. I have said good-bye to Benito on his leaving for Salzburg and told him to be careful about what he eats and talk frankly to Hitler. The Italians are prepared to fight on, but must have the wherewithal to do so and are tired of being the poor relation!"

CHAPTER XXIII

INVASION

"Second may, 1943. Benito is now paying for the strain of his journey to Salzburg. His old stomach pains are back and worse than ever. Dr. Pozzi wants another X-ray examination and Professor Bianchi approves, but I am sure it will reveal nothing new.

"6th May, 1943. Our troops in Tunis are putting up a splendid defence, but there is no hope left because our supply routes are blocked by the enemy's navy and air force. Even Mussolini is resigned to the inevitable. But after Tunis will it not be Italy's turn? That is the question which is so often on the tip of my tongue, but I have not had the courage to put it to my husband, as I do not wish to add to his tribulations.

"17th May, 1943. After the final news of the fall of Tunis we left Rome for la Rocca the other day. The renewal of the bombing is a terrible worry to Benito. He anticipates that the enemy will attempt an invasion of Sicily and the peninsula. Last night again he hardly slept at all. I know it is useless to try and console him with argument and better to leave him to his own thoughts. I sit quietly in my chair, as I know he likes having me about. Now and then he is called to the telephone or puts through a call himself. I can see his face darken at the news he gets; it is then that the deterioration of his health is really brought home to me. He has even been neglecting doctor's orders these days. When so much is at stake he has no heart to look after himself.

"18th May, 1943. Another sleepless night. I went into Benito's room while he was talking to Rome on the telephone and, as the conversation was a long one, I mechanically started a game of solitaire. All at once I noticed that Benito was standing behind me, closely following every move. What could he have been expecting from my simple diversion? I am dreadfully grieved about the fearful strain on him day and night.

"30th May, 1943. The Duce's official duties towards the government and the vital importance of recovering his health compel him to divide his time between Rome and the Rocca. On the 19th of last month he left for Rome, but was back again on the 26th. Today has been a black day, as the watchman found him lying on the floor, writhing with pain. The man rushed out of the room, horrified, and ran up to me shouting, 'The Duce is dying!' We immediately sent for Dr. Pozzi, who again began talking about another consultation. But the idea of too many doctors frightens me. Pozzi is now saying that even Frugoni's advice is not enough.

"The X-ray examination by Professor Puccinelli in Rome indicated the same diagnosis—gastritis and severe duodenal ulcers. Rest in bed and perseverance with the usual injections have been prescribed and the Duce has promised to obey.

"I was with him in Rome when the news of the fall of Pantelleria arrived. It was a terrible blow to him, though the air raids on the island had been heavy, and as a message had come from the garrison alleging that there was no water the High Command had authorised surrender. 'Do you know

what we have discovered from intercepted British reports?'
Benito asked me, with a wild look in his eyes. 'The garrison
of Pantelleria didn't lose one man! We owe all this to Admiral
Pavesi. He simply hoisted the white flag!'

"29th June, 1943. We have left Rome because the Duce
must receive the Rumanian representatives at the Rocca.
After three weeks in bed, he looks much better."

The Rumanian mission which came to Camminate was
headed by the Minister, Michael Antonescu, who presented
me with a gay Rumanian native dress.

The succession of reverses was a sore trial to the Italian
public and it was at this time that I suspected—and my
suspicions were partly confirmed from trustworthy sources—
that many people in high political and military circles were
at the head of a defeatist movement. Someone was certainly
betraying Mussolini and not a few were plotting against him
and the régime.

Among those conspirators were Dino Grandi, the President
of the Camera dei Fasci e Corporazioni and formerly Minister
of Justice (though at that time he was badgering the Duce
to get the Order of the Annunziata for him), Giuseppe Bottai
and Luigi Federzoni, President of the Italian Academy. It
also came to our ears that our son-in-law, Galeazzo Ciano,
was one of the group. For some time past my relations with
him had been strained. I did not approve of his mania for
mixing with some of the Roman aristocracy, from which both
Benito and I had always wanted to hold aloof. He often reproached me for "continuing to wear old-fashioned clothes
and remaining what I always was—a quiet, unassuming
woman". So we rarely met, and when we did our talk was
confined to conventional remarks. The news of his secret
opposition was reaching me from all quarters. One particular
sign of his unbounded ambition had been the way in which
he urged the promotion of Ettore Muti to the post of Party
Secretary, a post for which Muti was not suitable, as he was
essentially a typical soldier and not a politician.

General Soddu was also among those who were trying to
hide the truth from Mussolini. I particularly remember how
angry Mussolini was once when he told me that Soddu, when
in Greece, had sent in a report with specific instructions that
it should be kept secret from the Duce (to whom it was nevertheless shown by a loyal clerk). 'Whom can I trust?' my
husband groaned. Soddu was recalled and replaced.

Even Giuseppe Bastianini intrigued with Cavallero and company. I myself was informed that he had issued eleven passports to wives and women friends of the conspirators. (When Mussolini came to hear of the Cavallero plot, the plotters had feared the consequences and provided themselves with passports in case of flight.) Such was my information, but Bastianini denied everything when questioned by the Duce.

One day I decided to act on my own and sound Colonel Dolmann, Himmler's confidential envoy in Italy. A meeting was arranged at Buffarini's house and I discussed the situation with him. He agreed with me, but did not sound sincere. Later on I learned that he too could not be trusted.

I had to intervene several times to enable persons who had important things to say to the Duce or needed his help to get an interview, despite the obstacles put in their way by those wishing to keep him in the dark. Cases I can think of are those of the industrialist Pessina and Count Gianni Caproni, the well known industrialist and aeroplane builder.

The symptoms of a certain disintegration, which was mainly moral, were not confined to top circles. I opened my heart to Benito, urging him to be on his guard, but absorbed as he was in the ever increasing burden of work, with which he had to cope whenever his physical condition allowed, he refused to listen to me and kept saying, "Oh! those informers of yours!"

On top of the illness of which I have spoken, an old wound received on the Carso in 1917, which had reopened during the Ethiopian war and healed up again, began to trouble him after 1940, and seemed to defy treatment. That is why my husband was compelled to wear high boots with the opening down the back. I might say that though all his shoes looked as though they were laced, they were really elastic. He would not be bothered with doing them up.

Though Benito did not want to believe my accusations, and said my suspicions were unfounded, he admitted to an impression that his hands were increasingly tied. "In Rome there are three of us to give orders, the King, the Pope and myself," he used to say. "I can seldom do what I should like."

The first secret service reports about the Anglo-American plans to invade Sicily began to come in. Mussolini said that he was horrified at the idea of a part of the national territory being put to this supreme test, but added, "The reports from our generals—and I hope that they're hiding nothing this time—assure me that the invasion, if it comes, will meet with fierce resistance."

The history of the operations in Sicily is already well known, but I reproduce certain pages of my diary at that time in order to give a clear picture of the tragic days through which the family passed.

"10th July, 1943. I write these lines in the depths of despair, as I could not have believed that such a misfortune could overtake our country. Benito burst into my room shortly after dawn this morning, waking me up at once, as I am a light sleeper. 'Rachele, the Anglo-Americans have landed in Sicily,' he blurted out. I thought I was dreaming, but my husband was standing there before me, his face haggard. 'I'm sure our troops will put up a stout defence, and the Germans are sending reinforcements. We must have faith,' he added and left the room. I lay thinking about the uncertain future. If Sicily falls, shall we not see the enemy in the rest of Italy? My husband trusts the rank and file more than the generals, but if the generals are not competent—or are perhaps unwilling—to do their job, how can the army resist?

"18th July, 1943. I have just said good-bye to my husband who has left for a meeting with Hitler: he told me about it last night, though it did not seem to give him any satisfaction. His glowering looks told me what he means to say to his ally. He will be in Riccione tonight and tomorrow he will proceed to the meeting place.

"19th July, 1943. What Benito has been fearing for a long time—the bombing of Rome—has now happened. The danger has been hanging over us for several months, despite last winter's negotiations through the Vatican. Months ago I asked Benito, 'Why do they continue giving the alert in Rome?' 'Because they'll bomb Rome too some day, and the public must get used to going down into the shelters.' I replied that the Romans did not bother any more about these alerts because they were sure that the city would be immune. 'That may be, but one day they'll be disillusioned.'

"I was at the Villa Torlonia today, busy with my domestic duties as usual and I was not at all worried by the wail of the sirens. But all at once I heard the characteristic drone of aeroplanes flying low, and soon after a large number of explosions. The San Lorenzo quarter was particularly badly hit in the first wave. As the crow flies, it is little over a kilometre from the Villa Torlonia. It was only then that I decided to go down to the shelter with my maid and some workmen who were working in the villa. Then three bombs fell near the park, one of them quite near to a lodge. As soon as the all clear had sounded, I got into touch with the Ministry of the Interior and learned that there had been great damage and many casualties. In the afternoon I spent several hours in the linen room collecting as much linen and clothing as I could find to give to the homeless families. Later on Benito rang me up from Feltre. He was very worried about what had happened and anxious about me.

"20th July, 1943. Mussolini returned from Feltre last night. He arrived very tired after a day spent in the Veneto, while Rome was passing through tragic hours under bombardment. I know that it is a grievous blow to him because he loves Rome with a passion little short of morbid. He came home at about eleven o'clock looking quite haggard with weariness and his first questions were about the bombing. By now he knows from experience that I am the only one who tells him the truth which others try to hide from him. First thing this morning he went to pay his respects to the remains of General Hazon, the Commander of the Carabinieri, who is one of the victims. When he came back for lunch at two o'clock, he was very depressed about the scale of the disaster and furious because relief measures had not been organized in accordance with his orders by telephone from Feltre.

"22nd July, 1943. Benito is more worried than usual. After a long silence, and as if giving utterance to a decision he had been ruminating, he jumped up, looked me straight in the face and said, 'They want a meeting of the Grand Council; they shall have it! It's high time everyone should face up to his own responsibilities.' For the moment I said nothing, as I did not want to irritate him any further. Then, after a few hints from me, he continued, 'It's Grandi's and Federzoni's idea. They are always in it when dissension is about. But it won't make any difference.'

"Then he shut himself up in his study to work, and I am so weighed down with gloomy forebodings that I cannot bring myself to go to bed."

CHAPTER XXIV

PLOTS

IT WAS the evening of 20th July. Mussolini was dressing and the maid was fastening his collar. I had received very serious news about the intrigues of Badoglio, Ciano, Grandi and company. I reminded him that Badoglio had been tapping the telephones of the Villa Torlonia for some time and he replied, with a laugh, "Rachele, I'm worrying about the American tanks, not about Badoglio's listening-in or the intrigues of the others." I went on to say that I had received the list of names of the persons to whom Bastianini had given passports for abroad, but my husband remarked, with some irritation, that it was I who was the mischief maker. Then I took up the receiver, rang up Bastianini, raised the subject of the passports, gave him the actual names of those who had received them and told him that it was I who had informed Mussolini. The conversation went on until Benito took the receiver from me. This was only four days before the meeting of the Grand Council. Of this meeting I have the following notes in my diary:

"24th July, 1943. I rose this morning after an extremely disturbed night in which I hardly closed my eyes. I went off for a bit just before dawn, and then the bright summer sun suddenly woke me up. I knocked at Benito's door. He too was up. 'Is today's meeting really necessary?' I blurted out. He looked at me rather surprised: 'Why do you ask? I think it will only be clearing the air between friends; I don't see why we shouldn't have it.' Then I really flared up: 'Friends! Can the gang of traitors round you, Grandi first and foremost, be called friends? Do you know that Grandi has been missing for some days?' At the mention of Grandi's name he looked startled, but soon recovered his composure and tried to prove me wrong. But we parted each sticking to our own opinions. I am more than ever convinced that this meeting should not take place. While I am writing these notes in my room in a spare moment, Benito is at the Palazzo Venezia as usual. He honestly believes that everything will turn out for the best this evening, although he did admit the other day that there would certainly be a lively debate. A few days before the meeting at Feltre, Benito received circum-

stantial information about Ciano's secret contacts with other
members of the opposition in the Grand Council. Against
my express advice, Benito handed the text of the note to Scroza
at an interview at the Villa Torlonia, and ordered the Secretary of the Party to summon Ciano to give his explanation.
It was thus that this incriminating document came to the
knowledge of the interested parties and Ciano duly appeared
before the Duce to deny the accusations and proclaim his
loyalty. At this hour, Benito is receiving reports as usual at the
Palazzo Venezia. I hope the future will prove me wrong.

"Ten o'clock. Everything at lunch was as usual. In the
afternoon he got up and kissed me at the door of the villa.
He was carrying under his arm the file of documents and
while he was going towards his car, I turned round and
offered a suggestion, 'Have them all arrested before the opening!' And now I am faced with a long and trying wait.

"Twelve o'clock and no news. I rang up De Cesare at the
Palazzo Venezia and was told that the meeting was still going
on. Of course, I could hardly expect that such an important
meeting could be short. I could not master my feelings all the
same.

"25th July, 1943. 2 a.m. I rang up De Cesare four times.
No news. What was going on there? I never stopped thinking.
My thoughts went back to the remote past, to the first difficult
years of our married life and I realized that they were the
happiest. De Cesare called up at 3 a.m. He said he thought
the end of the meeting was in sight, but when I asked him
to tell me something about it his answer was vague. He told
me of the arrival of General Chierici, Chief of Police, and the
news relieved me.

"Five a.m. I am tired with the strain of keeping awake, but
it is nothing to the weight on my mind. It must have been
four o'clock when Benito returned home. I had already been
told that he had left the Palazzo Venezia. I was waiting up
for him and ran into the garden to meet him. He had Scorza
with him. His haggard, woe-begone face showed how things
had gone. I do not know what made me blurt out, 'You've
had them all arrested, I suppose?' Scroza gave me a surprised
look and Benito answered in low tones, 'No, but I will!' 'If
it's not too late,' I murmured. He sent the Party Secretary
back and handed me some papers. I followed him to his
study and then we gazed at each other in silence: in moments
of grief we understand each other without many words. He

was worn out. I asked him whether he wanted anything. 'Ring up the Supreme Command. I want to know whether there have been any alerts or bombings.' I had already made telephone inquiries in various quarters and knew that there were alerts at Bologna, Milan and many other Italian towns and some raids were in progress. But the Supreme Command merely answered, 'All is quiet, Duce. Nothing new to report on any part of national territory.' I heard what was said, snatched the receiver from my husband's hand, and yelled into the telephone, 'You're lying! The alert has been given in nearly all the cities in Italy. Why do you go on deceiving him?' Mussolini then called up the Prefect of Bologna and learned that in that city there had been continuous alerts since four o'clock. His face clouded over again and he murmured, 'There's nothing more I can do: they're set on our ruin. I'm afraid my orders don't count any more.' I understood his bitterness and let him go on talking. He told me all that had happened at the Great Council (it took him nearly twenty minutes). I only interrupted him once when he said that Galeazzo had sided with the opposition. 'He too!' I cried, shocked to the core, thinking that though life has its trials, great and small, for all of us, and they may come in mysterious ways, there are times when the burden seems too hard to bear.

"It was nearly five o'clock when we parted, wishing each other a good rest, but well knowing that neither of us would get any sleep."

(Long after the 25th July, 1943, a memorable day in the history of Italy, Mussolini told me at Salo that he was convinced, and always had been, that the Italian people had never taken any direct and effective part in the government crisis. It was the King who, inspired by personal and dynastic considerations, had yielded to the persuasions of the men around him, the leaders in the council, heads of high finance, and certain Fascist big-wigs who were alarmed at the turn of events in the war. It was the King who gave the signal for the course of action, devised and carried out in a manner far from regal, which had such catastrophic consequences. It was on such occasions that Benito bitterly reminded me how he had always tried to collaborate loyally with the monarchy, despite his preference for a republic, whilst the House of Savoy displayed all the outward signs of devotion and even subservience, while secretly cherishing a feeling of enmity calculated to create distrust and leave him with a sense of isolation, especially during the war.)

Yet only the day after the meeting of the Grand Council, Mussolini was absolutely sure that the King would reassert the Crown's trust in him, thereby enabling him to deal firmly with the conspirators. I did not share his confidence. I think he relied too much on appearances, and it must be admitted that the long series of telegrams of adulation and congratulations which the King and the Prince were always sending to their "Dear Cousin", and their visits to Rocca delle Camminate, were some justification. I attached more importance to hints of the King's ill-will which reached Mussolini from various quarters from time to time. I was impressed, for instance, by an incident at Castelporziano when one of the guards wrote him a letter warning him to beware of the King, whom he described as "timorous and untrustworthy" and after some rather picturesque remarks about the King ended: "His Majesty is afraid you may become too powerful, because the people love you too much." Mussolini had laughed and then forgotten all about it. But not I, because I knew other things as well—among them the circumstantial charges made to me on 8th May by one of the Queen's ladies-in-waiting, who arrived a little late for an audience. She gave me a full account of what she had seen and heard. Some of the things she noted surpassed my worst suspicions.

I also knew that Princess Maria Jose had been particularly hostile for some time, perhaps ever since the days when she wrote two very friendly letters to my husband, whom she had met at Castelporziano. It was at the moment of the conquest of the Empire, when the Princess made no secret of her approval of Mussolini.

CHAPTER XXV

ARREST AT THE VILLA SAVOIA

PREFECT ALBINI was then the Under-Secretary of the Interior. When he was called to fill the post in the winter of 1943 I reminded my husband of the numerous complaints which had been received on account of the irregularities committed by him when he was the Prefect of Naples. Mussolini had

(*Right*) The Duce and the King of Italy on army manœuvres

(*Below*) Mussolini and his two elder sons at the time of the Abyssinian War

(*Above*) Clara Petacci in her boudoir at the villa which Benito Mussolini built for her

(*Left*) Mussolini's private study in the Villa Torlonia

answered, "It is true, Rachele, but I choose my men in groups and among the good you get the bad . . . just as with apples. Besides, I hope that his new responsibility will induce him to redeem his past."

Someone had certainly informed Albini of my misgivings, because immediately after his appointment he asked to be received by me: at first I decided to refuse his request, but later decided to confront him frankly and spoke without reserve, as had been my practice with others of his type. I told him very clearly that our personal interests were a very small thing in comparison with the good of the nation; I reminded him of the sacrifices which the people had made; I spoke to him of my husband's hard work. He doggedly repeated all the usual stereotyped assurances of loyalty such as: "But, Madam, I am ready to give even my life," and "But, Madam, we all love the Duce," and so on. However, I gathered from his evasive attitude that I had spoken to no effect. Later I heard that he used to go to Castelporziano with Ciano, Prince Umberto and others who were plotting the *coup d'état*. It was about this that a lady-in-waiting was keeping me informed. And this man was responsible for Benito's arrest.

The pace of events prevented me from writing my diary on 25th July. I was far too worried. But even today I am able to reconstruct the phases of that day accurately.

When I got up on the morning of 25th July, after a few hours of broken sleep, Mussolini was already up. Dr. Pozzi came for the usual injection, but Benito would not have it. He was in a hurry. At eight o'clock he left Villa Torlonia to go to Palazzo Venezia and from there he sent for Grandi and Federzoni, but they were nowhere to be found. Shortly before eleven, the former Under-Secretary of the Interior, Guido Buffarini Guidi, rang me up to say he wanted to see me, and I realized that he did not want to say any more through the telephone. I fixed an appointment for five o'clock. Benito left Palazzo Venezia at two o'clock and reached home rather late. I was beginning to get anxious, when I recognized the unmistakable sound of the engine of his car. I went downstairs to meet him in the garden. In a few words he told me that he had been to visit the bombed areas of San Lorenzo and the Tiburtino, quarters inhabited exclusively by workmen, all poor people suddenly stricken both morally and materially. Yet, among all that horror, the people had received the Duce

9

with demonstrations of affection. It had been otherwise when
the King visited them a few days previously.

While we were going into the dining-room, he told me
that in the afternoon he was to see the King. He had nothing
but a little soup. Taken aback by this statement, I said,
"You must not go!" "I'm a man of honour," he replied, "we
have a pact with Germany to which we cannot be false. The
King signed it too and we must discuss the matter together.
If necessary, I shall remain at the head of the services to see
that we keep our word. It is a sad moment, Caporetto all
over again, but we can save the situation. But I may transfer
command to the King, provided he empowers me to arrest
the traitors." We finished our meal in silence. Then Benito
went into his study to look for some papers and came out
with a file which included a letter from Cianetti, one of the
members of the Grand Council, who had voted against him
and subsequently regretted it. He gave the papers to me and
I kept them all, including Cianetti's letter which later proved
of vital importance to his defence at the Verona trials.

Meanwhile the Palace had rung up no less than three times
to emphasise that Mussolini must appear in mufti instead of
uniform. Benito went to his room to change. Then the Private
Secretary, De Cesare, arrived at the Villa and I turned to
him saying, "I'm afraid you won't come home tonight." But
De Cesare too found my anxiety absurd. Then Benito came
down. My heart sank as I said good-bye and I stood at the
door of the villa until the car left, followed by the escort car.

At about five o'clock Buffarini arrived. He was still full of
the all-night sitting of the Grand Council and described the
course of events, telling me of Grandi's insolence and the
hostile attitude of Ciano and other members. He gave me
a sheet of paper on which the Duce had nervously doodled
during the sitting. Just when Buffarini, in the further course
of his story, had reached Scorza's speech, I was called to the
telephone. I ran to pick up the receiver and at once heard a
voice I knew talking in a frightened whisper, "They've just
arrested the Duce!" Although the announcement only confirmed my fears, I was petrified, so much so that Buffarini,
who had come over to me and was horrified at my expression,
took the receiver himself. "But who are you?" he kept repeating. "I can't tell you any more; don't lose a moment but warn
the children at Riccione." It was true that my family were
then at Riccione, where the person who was telephoning also

had some relations. I had wished to stay at my husband's side.

After the first terrible moment of anguish, we at once rang up the Command Headquarters of the Militia and the German Embassy, but no one knew anything, or would believe what we were telling them. Twice I rang up General Galbiati, but always with the same result. He said the story was impossible because "the city is absolutely calm."

Buffarini began to seem extremely alarmed; he made several telephone calls, was at a loss what to do and ended by staying in the villa all night, becoming increasingly worried and frightened until, at about one o'clock the next day, the Questore, called in by Buffarini himself under a previous arrangement, came in person to arrest him.

At about six o'clock we heard lorries drawing up and I thought that Benito's fate would be mine too, but all that happened was that some carabinieri appeared and ordered the police guard to leave on the lorries. Some of the police wanted to come in to say good-bye to me, but the carabinieri officer would not allow them to do so. Then they all went away leaving only a policeman on guard and two unarmed telephone operators. If the demonstrators who later thronged the streets of Rome had wished to kill me and loot the villa, they would have found nothing to stop them.

Left alone with my thoughts in turmoil, and Buffarini in a state of distraction, I spent the long hours of the evening and the night in ever-growing anxiety to know more of what had occurred. What had happened to Benito? At one point the boys rang me up from Riccione. My heart leaped when I heard Romano's voice. Cheery as ever and blissfully unconscious of what was afoot, he asked me if he could go to the cinema. As I was afraid that the telephone was being tapped, I limited myself to a few vague allusions to what had happened, but they were not understood. The children thought that I was trying to warn them of an imminent air raid on Riccione. They just laughed and rang off. At about ten o'clock, at our request, Questore Agnesina, until then the Duce's personal security officer, and Prefect Stracca arrived, and at last I was able to learn some further details. Agnesina had tears in his eyes as he gave them to us. We only knew that in the early afternoon Villa Savoia had sent for an extra squad of carabinieri. This, however, had happened before. Just before five o'clock Mussolini had entered the Villa and been told he was under arrest. As his car was still in the garden at a late hour, Agnesina presumed that Mussolini was still detained there. Buffarini, his secretary and I heard the story out and shortly after the two men had left we also heard the first radio announcement that Mussolini had been replaced by Badoglio.

During the night the shouts of the crowd, worked up by the sudden turn of events, penetrated to the inner rooms of the Villa Torlonia. In the morning a bellowing mob collected at the gate. I was not at all afraid. All I wanted was to know where Benito was. I was frantic with worry whether he was still alive, though an inner voice mysteriously assured me that he was not dead. I had seen him defying danger so often. How often had his life been attempted in vain? He was fond of saying, "I'm not easy to kill."

Everyone around was urging me to move from the Villa to a watchman's lodge near by, and it was there that Benito's housemaid, overcome by the tension, suddenly told me of the recent relations between my husband and a certain Clara Petacci, relations of which I knew nothing, though I had heard, sometimes from himself, about some previous affairs of the kind. I reproached the woman for having kept the information to herself and only disclosing it at such a moment. Naturally I was extremely worried at the news, though it was nothing to my anxiety about my husband's fate.

I remained in that state of ignorance all that night, the next day and the night following, in fact until the morning of Tuesday the 27th, when a young woman friend of mine decided to find out for herself what the real position was. With that object in view, she got into touch with Princess Mafalda d'Assia, who was a friend of hers and gladly told her what she knew. I was thus duly informed that my husband was alive, well and not in danger. My young friend added that from what the Princess said she had gathered the impression that the King was beginning to doubt whether he had acted rightly and that the Royal family's views on the matter were divided. The Princess had said she was very ashamed of what had happened and she very kindly kept us posted.

On Wednesday three hundred soldiers and some armoured cars arrived at the Villa Torlonia. In the afternoon I met the officer in command, who, without knowing who I was, asked me whether I had any news of the Mussolini family. Evidently he had not been told that I was still in the Villa, and it was I of all people whom he asked for details of the alleged arrest of Donna Rachele, which had taken place—so rumour had it—in Milan, where she had been found just as she was leaving for Spain with loads of jewels and trunks full of furs. I replied that I knew nothing at all and then complied with his request to show him round the Villa. He had passed through some of the rooms, showing great interest and asking me many questions about the Duce's family life, when we went into a room on the first floor, where an oil painting of Bruno in his pilot's uniform was very conspicuous. "I knew Bruno as a boy!" he exclaimed. "We were at school together in Milan. He was always cheerful and unaffected. I always admired him." He stood staring at the picture and apparently reviving old memories. "Did you know him?" he asked. With my son's picture before me my eyes filled with tears, partly because these were the first kind words I had heard after so many days of humiliation. The officer suddenly realized the situation and apologized. "I could not have believed that you would still be here, and alone," he said in his embarrassment.

CHAPTER XXVI

PRISONERS AT THE ROCCA

THE OFFICERS and soldiers treated me with every possible consideration; they went about the house quite quietly, apparently rather disappointed that everything was so simple and that the furniture was anything but grand. Many of them overcame their first shyness and came up to talk to me about their experiences during the war years and their family worries. They deplored the recent turn of events and, when they were leaving, always asked me for a small memento of the Duce.

An officer who introduced himself as Baron C. of Florence said, "We know where the Duce is. I'm in a position to tell you that he's alive, because my brother, who is stationed in a carabinieri barracks, has seen him." He was quite emotional when he gave me this news, and added that he believed that the Duce's imprisonment would not last very long.

"29th July, 1943. Today, Thursday, is Benito's birthday. A year ago we were together at the Rocca. Where are they

hiding him now?" It is with that mournful question that I
started writing my diary on a day so dear to my family. But
there were some other entries to come. "At last I have received
direct and official news of Benito, in the shape of a letter from
him personally which was delivered to me by a General Pòlito,
who arrived at the villa with two senior carabinieri officers.
He writes: 'Dear Rachele, the bearer will tell you what I
need. You know what the state of my health allows me to
eat, but do not send me much: only a few clothes—I haven't
any—and some books. I cannot tell you where I am, but can
assure you that I am all right. Don't worry and give my love
to the children. Benito.' These few lines tell me that he is
closely guarded, but still alive. I am slightly relieved, but far
from easy in my mind. What are they going to do with him.
I was given another letter to read, but I cannot quote it
verbatim, as I should have liked, because General Pòlito only
showed it to me and then took it back. It was from Badoglio
who asked me very formally to send clothes and money for
Mussolini, as otherwise he could not provide him with food.
This letter made me very angry. I reminded Pòlito that for
twenty years Mussolini had refused titles and rewards, and
given away all his presents from Italians and foreigners. I
said that it was intolerable that Badoglio, who had made a
fortune under the Fascist régime, should deny a crust to a
prisoner like this. At this outburst, my audience looked extremely uncomfortable until the carabinieri colonel, after
diverting the General's attention, took me aside and said in a
low voice, 'Madam, you are quite right. I cannot do much
unfortunately, but you can count on my loyalty. Try and keep
calm, because there are some people capable of anything, but
I understand and share your sorrow.' As he spoke, he showed
me the Fascist badge which he kept under the lapel of his
coat. I have sent Benito a nice parcel of small, but useful and
welcome things which will help to make his imprisonment
more bearable. The books included Ricciotti's *Life of Christ*,
which I found open on his desk.

"30th July, 1943. General Pòlito has left and at last I have
remembered who he is: I met him at Bologna when he was
treasurer there and professed to be an admirer of Mussolini
and an ardent Fascist. I remember him as a humble official
who felt himself honoured to carry 'Donna Rachele's suit-case'.
Now he is called General, though I don't know of which
corps. He tried to comfort me with news of my children, who

are still at Riccione, and regretted that I could not talk to them on the telephone because the lines were blocked."

On the last day of July and the first of August nothing appears in my diary, though I remember that I had two more visits from General Pòlito, who was anxious to make history in his own way, and a few cautious visits from faithful friends who told me of the utter disillusionment of the people after the delirium of the first moment. I was simply living in hopes of receiving another letter from Benito and news of my children. I wandered round the deserted rooms of the villa : in the children's rooms there was a silence which seemed nothing more than an interval between their shouts of laughter. A mouth-organ and some open books were lying about, just as if they might come in at any moment. In the Duce's room the files and documents he spent all his time in studying were strewn about just as he had left them. What was happening to him now? Would we ever be together again? How often when I had sat silently sewing at his side while he wrote had I thought of a tranquil old age to be spent, not in the noise and bustle of Rome, but in the cosy intimacy of Rocca delle Camminate! And now everything seemed to have crumbled to dust.

"2nd August, 1943. According to General Pòlito I am leaving tonight for the Rocca. He has assured me that I shall find my children there. I got together a few things in that gentleman's presence, so that he should see what I was leaving and what I was taking with me : a service kit-bag and, my only valuables, my husband's decorations. Left alone once more, I wandered about the house, the sweet kingdom I had so firmly ruled for so many years. The soul of every woman is inseparable from her home and I, a true daughter of the Romagna, have always been intensely conscious of it. My children had come here as tots and, when they were grown up, gone away to start new families. Here it was that I said good-bye to Bruno whom fate had taken from me so soon. Here, after so many years of happiness for ourselves and the Italian nation, I had passed through the grievous years of war. My heart aches when I think about the past and ask so many questions about the future. The poignancy of my leaving was increased by the good wishes of some loyal gendarmes just as I was realizing my isolation."

The drive from Rome to the Rocca was dreadful. Once again my companions were Pòlito and the carabinieri colonel,

who sat beside the chauffeur. We could have easily reached
the Rocca in six or seven hours, but Pòlito was so intent on
avoiding main roads that we took more than twelve hours.
On the way we saw foreign propaganda leaflets in favour of
Badoglio being distributed.

We left towards eleven o'clock on the night of 2nd August.
The General smoked cigars continuously and it was absolutely
suffocating in the car with all the windows up. I thanked
God when, at eleven o'clock in the morning, I caught sight
of the distant tower of the Rocca, bathed in sunshine. I was
safe and sound and would very shortly be home. I saw that
carabinieri were mounting guard outside as usual. All was
quiet and I could almost have imagined that the events in
Rome were a bad dream had it not been for the ache in my
heart for Benito. Romano and Anna Maria were already at
the Rocca and they gave me news of our other relations at
Riccione. The General left in a hurry, deferential to the end.
I restrained the expressions of contempt which were on the
tip of my tongue and hardly said good-bye.

Then a period of isolation began. In accordance with the
orders issued, we were not allowed to leave the park or go
near the gates. The carabinieri were under orders to shoot if
we disobeyed. Even visits from friends wishing to see us were for-
bidden. During the whole time—several weeks—we remained
at the Rocca, I received only four letters from my husband.
He said little about himself, but was eager for news of his
children. The letters had been opened when they reached me.
From the way he wrote I realized that he did not know what
had happened. He was under the impression that the Rocca
had been badly damaged and that our nephew Vito was with
us, whereas in fact I did not know where Vito was. I answered
him that he was still being kept in the dark. He told me,
among other things, that he had been prevented from being
present at the memorial mass on the anniversary of Bruno's
death. The authorities of Forli refused me permission also and
on that sad occasion I was not even able to visit the nearby
cemetery of S. Cassiano, where my son is interred. Of course
the telephone was not working and nothing but occasional
and fragmentary news reached us from outside. During the
sunny August afternoons Anna Maria read and Romano
played the piano, though he had to do without a teacher.

We had something to do when we found ourselves concerned in the fate of forty-five children evacuated from Genoa

whom we had taken into our house at Carpena. We had always
looked after them and the cost of their maintenance up to the
end of August had been provided for, but now they seemed to
be forgotten. After much persuasion, I was able to get the
municipal treasurer of Forli to come and see me at the Rocca.
Arrangements were not easy to make, but I persisted until I
had got the children transferred to the colony at Predappio,
which already belonged to the G.I.L.

Somewhere about the beginning of September, after the
enemy landing in Calabria, our situation grew worse because
we were more closely guarded. On the evening of 8th September, a carabinieri N.C.O. told me the disastrous news of
the armistice. Our beautiful valleys resounded with the ringing of bells, and the bonfires lit during the night seemed to
me mournful funeral pyres when I thought in sorrow of the
useless sacrifice of so many lives and how many mothers had
suffered in vain. I wondered what would become of Italy and
Mussolini. Where and how would he have heard the terrible
news?

Four days later there was a dramatic turn in the situation.
At about ten o'clock in the morning of 12th September, some
German officers and soldiers suddenly appeared at the Rocca
delle Camminate. The carabinieri were disarmed and placed
themselves at their disposal. The N.C.O. who had been so
overbearing was now as meek as a lamb. Shortly afterwards
the German officers introduced themselves to me. They showed
considerable emotion and asked me to get ready to leave with
the children almost at once. When I inquired their reasons,
they said that all they knew was that our destination was
Vienna.

Romano, Anna Maria and I lost no time in getting ready.
I did not know what lay ahead, but we all felt that it was
going to be something good. By the early afternoon we were
already at Forli airfield. We flew in a fully armed bomber,
which was escorted by another plane. Over Verona the pilot
changed direction, as we were heading for an enemy air
formation. A cloud screen helped us to escape the danger,
but meanwhile the weather had become worse and we had
to land at Munich instead of Vienna. We were accommodated
at the Hotel Vierjahreszeiten.

After dinner a senior German introduced himself, stood to
attention, and announced in a voice quivering with emotion,
"I have good news for you, Donna Rachele Mussolini; our

airmen have rescued the Duce from his prison on the Gran
Sasso. The Duce is already on his way to Vienna."

Romano and Anna Maria were wildly excited and smothered
me with kisses. The strain of these last few days gave way to
a happy relief we could hardly credit, so miraculous the whole
thing seemed. Now I could understand the sudden order to
leave the Rocca; while Hitler was arranging Benito's rescue,
he had had a thought for us as well; he would save us from
possible retaliation on the part of the Badoglio gang. Romano
and Anna Maria, all impatient, tried to get further details out
of some German officers they met in the hall. They both knew
German, but their bashfulness and excitement prevented them
from making themselves too well understood.

Eventually, on the morning of the 13th, we were told that
a plane was leaving Vienna with the Duce on board and we
would be seeing him in Munich very soon, as he would land
there for a short time before continuing his journey to meet the
Fuehrer at General Headquarters. His plane was expected to
arrive at two o'clock and at that hour we were at the airport
to await his arrival. The thought of being able to embrace
Benito once more after all that had happened seemed like a
dream. When the three aeroplanes came into view and touched
down a little later, we could hardly contain our feelings. The
German civilians fell on their knees as if they were seeing a
ghost while the military stood stiffly to attention.

CHAPTER XXVII

RESCUE OF THE DUCE

"THIRTEENTH SEPTEMBER, 1943. I had expected to find Benito
very exhausted, but when he walked up to us in his usual
sprightly fashion, his deathly pallor gave me a dreadful shock.
He was wearing the ski-ing boots and very shabby black suit
I had sent him from the Rocca, where I kept only old clothes I
put aside to give to the poor. 'I didn't think I should ever see
you again,' were his first words, and then, after hugging each
other, we found ourselves speechless for a bit before we remembered that he was to resume his journey almost immediately
and moved off to the airport controller's private room where

we could talk freely. We had a lot to tell each other about the dreadful days of separation, all that had happened in Italy and his rescue. It sounds incredible, but he was still quite in the dark about the situation in Italy after 25th July. He was very bitter about the treachery of men whom he believed loyal, and very pleased when I told him that not all had deserted him. 'What do you intend to do now,' I asked him. He looked at me in silence for a moment and then talked very fast, as if afraid I might interrupt or argue with him, 'I shall have to have a long talk with Hitler, but I'm determined not to abandon my course of action, and to do what may still be possible to save the Italian people.' I gazed at him for a few minutes. There were many things I wanted to say but confined myself to a question, 'Do you really think it's worth while?' 'I know it may cost me my life,' he answered, 'but I'll keep my word. The 8th September will certainly prove a fateful day for Italy and now more than ever we must stick by our ally.'

"At that moment the Airport Controller came in to tell us that the bad weather would not allow Benito to continue his journey. Benito could not go on to General Headquarters before tomorrow. Of course this little contretemps has delighted us. We got into the car, thinking of all we still had to say to each other."

The temporary residence put at Mussolini's disposal was got ready remarkably quickly. It had been the Karl Palatz, one of Munich's most beautiful buildings. The news of the Duce's presence spread like lightning and the hall of our suite was always crowded with German officers and distinguished civilians, as well as Italians clamouring for a personal interview to demonstrate their loyalty. Among these Italians was a very large number of workmen.

I was soon busy getting a bath ready for Benito, who badly needed it. He had not had a change of clothes for some time and his socks were sticking to his feet. When he saw the bedroom fit for a prince that had been prepared for him, he took fright and chose to sleep with me in my more homely room. We kept together until the late hours listening to the Fascist broadcast from Munich giving the latest news of the Italian situation. Then Benito told us the story of his arrest, the forty-five days in prison and his wonderful rescue.

"14th September, 1943. The Duce left at eleven o'clock this morning for the German General Headquarters. Last night he was talking to us for nearly two hours, partly because we interrupted him now and then to supplement his story with ours, and also because he had so much to say. Today, after a quiet night for once, I am trying to recall his exact words. It is his personal wish that I should put his story in writing. Romano too has made a note of part of what he said so that there shall be a true record of the more important incidents:

" 'His Majesty was at the door of the Villa Savoia. He seemed in a state of great agitation, so much so that his words were little more than a jerky, painful mumble. As we entered the study he began his attack, lapsing into Piedmontese dialect with the statement that things were going badly and the soldiers did not want to fight for me any longer. Then, biting his nails, he became more specific: "At this moment you are the most hated man in Italy and have but one friend you can count on; your one last friend is—myself." Then he told me that he meant to replace me with Badoglio, who was to form a government of civil servants to conduct the business of the country and continue the war. "A temporary solution," he added, "for the next six months; then we shall decide what is to be done." I did not lose my temper. I admitted that I had realized, as I said at the Grand Council, that the people hated me—no one could govern so long and exact so many sacrifices without provoking ill-will, passing or permanent. However, I wished luck to the man who was going to succeed me. The conversation lasted about twenty minutes. The King accompanied me to the door and shook hands with me. While I was walking towards my car, deep in thought, I was stopped by a carabinieri officer. "His Majesty has charged me with your personal safety," he whispered. At first I did not take in what he said and went on walking to my car; but then the officer pointed to a motor ambulance near by and told me that I was to get in. I got in and found myself in the company of De Cesare and several armed carabinieri. The ambulance moved off at high speed.

" 'I still thought that all this had actually been arranged by the King for my protection and considered all these precautions exaggerated. But never for a moment did I doubt the King's word. When I got out of the car at the Carabinieri Cadet Barracks, I began to realize the true position. Everyone seemed very excited. I was taken to the Commandant's room, where I settled down as best I could. Next morning, when I noticed many armed sentries in the corridor and courtyard,

I knew I was a prisoner. Later on I received a letter from Badoglio. It ran as follows: "To His Excellency Cavaliere Benito Mussolini. The undersigned Head of the Government wishes to inform Your Excellency that what is being done as regards your person is solely in your own interests, in view of specific information from several quarters of a serious plot against your life. He therefore wishes to inform you that he will give orders that you shall be safely escorted, with all due consideration, to anywhere you may indicate. The Head of the Government: Badoglio, Marshal."

" 'The story about my personal safety continued. I at once dictated the following answer: "26th July, 1943, 1 o'clock. (1) I thank Marshal Badoglio for his concern for my personal safety. (2) The only residence at my disposal is the Rocca delle Camminate, where I am prepared to go at any time. (3) I desire to assure Marshal Badoglio, recalling our work together in days gone by, that there will be no difficulty on my side and I will co-operate in every way. (4) I am glad of the decision taken to continue the war with our ally, as the honour and the interests of the country require at this moment, and it is my heartfelt desire that success shall attend the grave task which Marshal Badoglio is undertaking in the name and on the order of H.M. The King, whose faithful servant I have been for twenty years, and still remain. Long live Italy!"

" 'I received no reply. On the morning of 27th July there was much coming and going in the barracks, which continued until the evening. At about eight o'clock General Pòlito, Chief of Police at G.H.Q., presented himself and announced that I must leave. This curious General had no difficulty in admitting that Fascism had "made" him, and during the journey told me many incidents in his police career. I really thought we were going in the direction of Rocca delle Camminate, but after about an hour, despite the drawn blinds, I noticed that the car was travelling south. The first stop was Gaeta. The corvette *Persefone* was waiting in the port, and as soon as we were on board, it headed towards Ventotene. On the way a further order was received, perhaps because there was a small German garrison at Ventotene, and the corvette made for Ponza. During the voyage there were some sympathetic demonstrations by the sailors. Going up on deck I noticed the words, "Courage, Duce, we are with you" scrawled on the side. A sailor came up to me and said, "Duce, I've heard you are short of money. Allow me to offer you my savings." He produced four hundred lire and I accepted them, because the fact was I hadn't a cent. Shortly afterwards another sailor brought me some underwear, and who knows how much longer this charitable rivalry would have continued had not the Commandant of the ship "invited" me to retire to my cabin.

" 'Nor were there any hostile manifestations at Ponza. To the amazement of the carabinieri sergeant-major who had me in charge, I was quartered in a low, damp little house on the shore. It was a lonely spot, but the kindly attentions I received from the inhabitants made me forget the bitterness of solitude. My only great disappointment was that I was not allowed to attend the mass I had asked the parish priest of Ponza to say on the anniversary of Bruno's death. During the night of 17th August I was suddenly roused from sleep—we were to leave at once for Maddalena, though our actual destination was only made known at sea, in the middle of a very rough crossing.

" 'At Maddalena, I was handed over to Admiral Brivonesi. A small villa was put at my disposal. It was certainly not as miserable as my quarters at Ponza, but the atmosphere all around was menacing and hostile. The house was surrounded by soldiers and it was clear that a German *coup de main* was feared. In fact, the mere appearance of a German plane flying low over the roof of the villa was the signal for a further hurried exodus. In the meantime I had received the twenty-four volumes of the complete works of Nietzsche, a birthday present from Hitler, and incidentally the first sign of interest from outside (beyond a letter from you, Rachele). On 28th August, I arrived at the station of the Gran Sasso funicular and remained for a few days in a building nearby. Then I was transferred to the big hotel on the Campo Imperatore, a most unusual prison, three thousand metres above sea level.

" 'Although I was treated with every consideration, I was closely guarded. One concession was that I was allowed to listen to the radio and it was thus that I got my first news after weeks of isolation—news which was only scraps of information about what had happened and was pending in Italy, so that I was unable to reconstruct recent events. Only once did I leave the hotel, accompanied by a guard who had great trouble in keeping control of four wolfhounds who were also part of the prisoner's guard. The view from the top of the Campo, where the hotel stood, was very beautiful. At one moment, when my guardian had been dragged some distance away by the dogs, an old shepherd came up to me and murmured, "So it's really true that you're here, Duce. The Germans are looking for you everywhere in order to rescue you. I'll let them know where you are. When I tell my wife that I've seen you, she won't believe me." He was wearing a sheepskin coat and corduroy trousers, which gave him a sturdy, primitive air. He kissed my hand and disappeared.

" 'On the night of 8th September, after the announcement of the armistice over the radio, I was even more closely guarded. Two nights later I casually heard, on the radio, that one of the conditions of the armistice was that I should be handed over to the Allies. I swore that that could only be over my dead body and wrote a letter to that effect to Lieutenant Faiola, who was in command of the garrison. This officer came to my room at once and took away anything I might find useful if I wanted to commit suicide, though he assured me, with tears in his eyes, that he would never hand over an Italian to the English, as he had once been captured by the British himself.

" 'In the afternoon of 12th September, the amazing rescue took place. I was looking out of the window which looked straight down the valley. It must have been two o'clock, as I had just finished lunch. A glider suddenly alighted about one hundred metres from the hotel, and before I could speculate where it had come from I saw men in uniform running up. At first I thought they were British soldiers, but soon recognized the German uniforms. It was a quick business. The party at once set up machine-guns covering the hotel, while other gliders landed and lined up on the flat ground in front and all the men took up their positions with their weapons at the ready. In the corridor behind me I heard confused movement, shouts and orders, and below me parties of Germans were rushing towards the hotel so fast that the garrison had not time to organize a defence, even if it was so minded. But as there was a sound of preparations to fire, and it looked as if rifles might go off by themselves at any moment, I yelled from the window, "Can't you see there's an Italian General out there!" It was true. An officer in the grey-green Italian uniform was conspicuous among the first arrivals. It was General Soleti, who, as I learned later, had been brought as a hostage, and in fact had come voluntarily himself. It may be that my warning averted bloodshed. A few moments later a German officer burst into my room, his face beaming. He was Captain Skorzeny. I was overcome and fell on his neck thanking him, and with him Hitler, who had sent him. He told me all about the raid, and in particular that there had only been a few casualties, despite the hazardous landing. By now the carabinieri were fraternising with the Germans.

" 'There was no time to lose and I soon found myself on board a 'storch' airplane with the pilot and Captain Skorzeny. Taking-off was a tricky and risky business. The carabinieri stood round and waved good-bye. The whole thing had only taken one hour.' "

CHAPTER XXVIII

AT SCHLOSS HIRSCHBERG

WHEN MUSSOLINI went off on his visit to German G.H.Q., we were left to ourselves once more, and the children immediately started a round of sightseeing in Munich which impressed them greatly, for despite the first bombings it was still a beautiful city, with its great variety of Gothic and neo-classic buildings. The Gran Sasso exploit had caused a sensation, and the portraits of Mussolini and Hitler could be seen everywhere.

Benito phoned me late that afternoon from G.H.Q. He said he had had a long talk with the Fuehrer and was satisfied with the outcome of this first meeting. Hitler had been very concerned over my husband's health and insisted on his being treated by his personal physician. I was very pleased at this, because I was worrying about the effects of Benito's imprisonment on his health.

After supper that evening we were shown some documentary films in the main hall of the palace. The first one, showing Mussolini's rescue, was frantically cheered by the Germans, and we ourselves watched with growing emotion. As soon as we had retired to bed, the alert sounded and we had to make for the air-raid shelter. No bombing followed, however.

"18th September, 1943. Mussolini returned from G.H.Q. yesterday, after three days of intense work with Hitler. 'Intense work' is Benito's own description and I know what that means for him. He is rather tired, because confinement interrupted the routine of non-stop work to which he was accustomed. Physically

(*Right*) In characteristic mood; Mussolini speaking from a threshing machine at Aprilia, a new township in the reclaimed Pontine marshes

(*Below*) The wedding of Bruno Mussolini to Gina Ruberti. Donna Rachele is standing beside the bridegroom

A recent photograph of Donna Rachele Mussolini with her daughter Edda and grandson Fabrizio Ciano. They had been visiting Mussolini's tomb in the cemetery at Pradappio in 1957

he looks better and seems to be recovering rapidly, but there is a bitter expression in his eyes which betrays his mental torment. He hinted as much to me, and I can understand how the new situation in Italy embarrasses him in dealing with Hitler.

"Late in the afternoon he shut himself up to prepare a speech and afterwards broadcast on Munich radio his first address to the Italians since his rescue. I went with him into the little transmission room fixed up in the Karl Palatz. It may seem strange, but the fact is that this was only the second time he had broadcast. Hitherto his speeches were always made in public in the presence of his audience, though they were relayed by radio.

"He was not at his ease, and before he began his eyes held mine. After a pause, which it seemed would never end, he began to speak. At first his voice was low and tired, but as he went on his old fighting spirit returned. It may be that many of his hearers in Italy found it hard to recognize his voice. As soon as he had finished, he came up to me and said: 'I am convinced that Italy can still be saved. Those who believe in the cause, and the fighting men, will respond to my appeal.' "

In the days following he resumed his old habits of work, though he had little more than a pencil and a few sheets of paper. His first contacts involved an unending series of interviews. I used to ask him how he managed to carry on, and he would reply, "I suppose it's my destiny, Rachele."

Among those who rejoined the Duce and whom I came to know well in those days I remember Roberto Farinacci who gave Benito most encouragement and was always exhorting him to "be hard", De Cesare his private secretary, Buffarini, former Under-Secretary for the Interior, Candelori Riccardi, formerly a minister in the Treasury, our Vittorio and his friend Ruperti, and Filippo Anfuso, who gave the Duce a black shirt because he did not possess one. Alessandro Pavolini, Giovanni Preziosi, Cesare Rivelli, who all had been in Germany for some time, broadcasting from Radio Munich, had met the Duce at G.H.Q. I shall speak of the visit of Edda and Ciano later on.

Meanwhile the enemy air raids induced the Germans to invite us to move to Schloss Hirschberg. The castle is beautifully situated fifty miles south of Munich, in full view of the Bavarian Alps and Garmisch, the winter sports resort. From its walls we could sometimes see the glow of fires caused by the bombing of Munich.

Benito came with us and stayed on, in order to get on with his work. We had spent about a week at Munich.

The castle grounds and the building itself were cleverly camouflaged overnight, and there were no air attacks during the whole of our stay. (I have been told that Marshal Pétain subsequently occupied our rooms.)

In that secluded corner of Bavaria were made the plans for the Social Republic, which met with the approval of Marshal Graziani, many other important people and even some former opponents of the régime. "There must be an entirely new approach, with new men and ideas, profiting by our experience," my husband used to say. Nonetheless, as a result of German pressure, the top posts in the new Ministry and the reconstituted party were given to party leaders who had held office before 25th July and no longer enjoyed the confidence of Benito or the great majority. Attilio Teruzzi and Telesio Interlandi paid brief visits to the castle. Farinacci also reappeared and pressed for a portfolio. Benito declined and asked him to return to his native Cremona.

Towards the end of September Mussolini decided to go back to Italy. I was to remain in Bavaria with the children and join him a little later. The sudden decision upset me and I asked him whether it was really necessary for him to return. He had a ready answer, "Badoglio's declaration of war has placed Italy in an absurd position. I must go and see what's happening, and put relations between Italians and Germans on a proper footing."

With the little money I had brought from Italy and a contribution from some very close friends, we scraped together fifteen thousand lire, which was all Benito had when he left for Rocca delle Camminate. Pavolini was already in Rome, helping to draw up the constitution of the Republican Fascist Party and reconstruct a government.

While we were in Munich, Galeazzo Ciano with Edda and their three children, Fabrizio, Raimondo and Marzio, had settled in a villa, guarded by Germans, on a lake in the vicinity of Munich. Galeazzo had sent Edda to G.H.Q. to ask the Fuehrer for permission to move to Portugal and obtain the necessary currency. Hitler refused point blank, which resulted in the first clash between them. On Benito's return from his first visit to G.H.Q. she then appealed to him and insisted on his receiving Galeazzo. The painful meeting took place at the Karl Palatz in Munich, in the presence of Edda and myself.

Ciano defended himself against the charge of treachery and attacked Badoglio. Benito was very angry, but heard him out. Next day we all had lunch together, before Benito left for German G.H.Q. again. In the days following I met Galeazzo on several occasions and reproached him for his behaviour at the Grand Council, but he flatly denied that he had supported Grandi.

Edda went to Italy by herself, in order to clear her husband of the grave charges that were being made against him. To her amazement, she met with a hostile reception.

During the next few days Galeazzo had an operation on one of his ears, and when he returned to the villa by the lake, found that his children were no longer there. The German General Wolf had in fact, brought them to me at the castle. Galeazzo came looking for them and told me he proposed to return to Italy, as he hoped to be given a political post, and if that was not forthcoming, he had decided to join up as a pilot. As I was still unconvinced about his previous behaviour, he launched into a scathing denunciation of Badoglio, Cavallero, Grandi and Bottai. On learning that Cavallero had committed suicide, he remarked, "the best thing he could do." Meanwhile Edda was pleading her husband's cause with Benito at Rocca delle Camminate. Eventually the Germans answered that Ciano could fly to Italy, but on landing at Verona he found Italian and German police waiting for him and was arrested and thrown into the town gaol.

In that interval of comparative calm Romano and Anna Maria used to roam the country round Schloss Hirschberg and go climbing and fishing, sometimes nearly as far afield as Munich. I preferred to stay at the castle, which overlooked two small lakes. Our family group grew larger with the arrival of my daughter-in-law Orsola and her children. The Germans were wonderful hosts, and always treated us with the greatest courtesy. They once gave me a coupon for a very large ration of petrol. I was so amazed at the figure on the coupon that I sent for the officer who had brought it. "Please thank your superior, but I don't need the petrol," I said. "It's scarce and had better be kept for something more useful."

Benito used to ring me up every evening from the Rocca to get our news and then tell me about the day's doings at his end. "It's uphill work," he would often say, "but I shall succeed." I was not surprised at his optimism, though at first he had been much shaken by the state of affairs he had found in Italy.

"You were right," he used to say, "there's absolutely nothing left. It's like coming back after a hurricane."

The general situation was so serious that I often wondered how he could stand the strain. Our separation increased my fears and I felt that my company would be good for him, so I was delighted when he asked me to come home, as he did on the telephone one evening. I was on my way the very next day. We drove in a car, provided by the Fuehrer himself, with an escort.

I felt relieved when we reached the Brenner and I was once again on Italian soil. By 3rd November I was with Benito at the Rocca. He had just returned from a tour in the Lake Garda district, where it was proposed that the new G.H.Q. should be established. On the previous day he had visited the graves of his family and Bruno in the cemetery at S. Cassiano.

My first contacts with our neighbours revealed a general bewilderment so intense that the peasants themselves were not quite sure whether the man who had come back to the Rocca could really be Mussolini. On one occasion I was so annoyed that I took a local woman by the arm and led her to the study where my husband was. She could not help recognizing the Duce at once.

It gradually dawned on Mussolini and myself that the doubts about Mussolini's existence and the northern government were the result of propaganda from the south. It was obvious that many people did not believe he was still alive, either because they did not want to believe it or because it did not suit them to do so.

CHAPTER XXIX

ON LAKE GARDA

My husband was extremely pleased, and in fact thoroughly relieved at my return to the Rocca. He had missed me very much, as the business of housekeeping was too complicated without me. I got things straight and we spent many autumn evenings together while he was telling me how he was getting on with the establishment of the Republican government in Italy.

He had no money at all when I arrived. The fifteen thousand

lire I had handed to him at Munich had soon run out, and so had the eighty thousand lire, the proceeds of the sale of some furniture at the Villa Torlonia, which my daughter-in-law Gina, Bruno's widow, gave him. All this was a drop in the ocean, as we had to play host to the German officers of the unit guarding the castle, and there was nothing wrong with their appetites. When the stock of food and wine I had left behind on my departure for Germany ran out, Benito, who knew nothing about running a house, and had far more important matters to worry about, had left the housekeeping to the housemaid. Matters had now reached a crisis. I found myself in a quandary when I arrived but took over the reins with my usual vigour and was able to draw on some savings we had deposited. After a few awkward months our circumstances improved when Benito was able to hand over his author's royalties at Gargnano.

Then came the decision to transfer G.H.Q. and the entire government to Lake Garda. The choice was dictated by considerations of geography. Rome was no longer sufficiently central for the area governed by the Social Republic and Milan could not be considered because of air raids. So it was decided to disperse the ministries over small places with suitable buildings on and around Lake Garda.

We arrived at Gargnano on a sunny November afternoon, and found the mild air refreshing after what had been a windy drive over the Apennines. At Descenzano we suddenly came in full view of the lake, a huge blue mirror. The massive hump of Monte Baldo was already covered with snow, in strange contrast to the luxurious vegetation all round. We took up quarters in the Villa Feltrinelli at Gargnano; the rent had been fixed at eight thousand lire monthly. It is a handsome residence on the lake, standing in its park with an olive grove on one side. The building is covered with pink marble, which contrasts strongly with the rude masonry of a small tower, since demolished. The villa provided quarters for G.H.Q. as well for about a month, until the latter was transferred to the Villa delle Orsoline, almost in the centre of the district.

The house had been somewhat neglected and our first impression was not too favourable, but I immediately set about rearranging the furniture and got the place looking comfortable and homelike. There was not much room, however, and we were half submerged in the comings and goings of German soldiers who mounted guard alternately with our men and made the villa look more like a barracks. After a few days the German officers and men moved elsewhere, and we were left with some thirty men of the Duce's Guard, comprising mainly the pick of the Pesaro and Romagna contingents and a platoon of German S.S. The latter were subsequently removed too. But these security measures seemed excessive to Mussolini, and the police officials had their work cut out to fix up an arrangement which would not be too conspicuous. Nearly every day Benito went for a spin on his bicycle in the park and the guards did their best not to be seen, though he liked exchanging the time of day with them. We were, however, spared the sight of rifles in every corner and the house began to look almost normal.

It was then that we missed the children. Benito had always liked to see them around, especially at meal times. All the time we were alone we were reduced to eating at a small table in his bedroom. Eventually our children came back from Bavaria, and our grandchildren with them, and they considerably livened up the atmosphere.

Benito divided his day between the two villas. Once more he was as busy as he had been at the Palazzo Venezia; he worked even in the few hours he spent at home. He read newspaper articles and books, especially those on philosophical and historical subjects. From the beginning he was absorbed at home in the projected new constitution for the Republic and the "Eighteen Basic Points" which subsequently became the "Manifesto" approved by the Verona Assembly. He personally consulted the most famous jurists. The first draft of the constitution was the work of Carlo Alberto Biggini, but Mussolini found it unsatisfactory and Senator Roland-Ricci was called in to revise it. The Senator had never been a Fascist, but he contributed enthusiastically to its final shape.

Mussolini did a lot of writing. His old passion for journalism revived and he used to contribute articles to daily papers and the *Corrispondenza Republicana* (political notes on outstanding events, issued by the Stefani news agency). He also worked on his *History of a Year* which created so much interest with its revelations on the events of the 25th July.

When it was not raining he used to play tennis after his bicycle ride. Though long practice had made him a pretty good player, I was astonished at the fact that he nearly always won. My instinct proved right, as usual, and I soon discovered that his over-enthusiastic supporters had told his opponents to let him win. This was very embarrassing for him, so I encouraged him to take no notice and a stop was soon put to that nonsense.

Benito also liked going for walks with Romano, who was beginning to take an interest in current events. We used to have him with us when films were being shown. On one occasion we put on a documentary film, obtained through a neutral country, of the entry of the Anglo–American troops into Naples.

What my husband liked most about Anna Maria was her vivacity, and he had no objection to her frequent visits to the Villa delle Orsoline when she was not studying at home. Romano attended school at Desenzano. Vittorio, our nephew Vito, Vanni Teodorani and Renato Tassinari were employed in the Private Secretariat with Prefect Dolfin. The experiment proved none too successful, however, and was short-lived.

The village of Gargnano was very overcrowded, thanks to the presence of the Italo–German garrison, the comings and goings of the Republican Government personnel, military chiefs, ambassadors, journalists and persons of all categories summoned for an audience. The local population, mainly fishermen and labourers, was always friendly.

Enemy planes, both bombers and fighters, flew over the villa almost daily, especially in 1945, and also operated in the vicinity of Gargnano, though they never made it their target. An inconspicuous air-raid shelter had been built, but I could never prevail on my husband to use it, even when bombs were exploding nearby. I used to rap fiercely on his door, but the only answer I got was, "Not every Italian has a shelter to go to."

The entries in my diary during the early days of the Social Republic are largely concerned with the trial of those members of the Grand Council who had been responsible for the collapse of the régime. That trial was an unending nightmare.

First and foremost, there was the personal position of Galeazzo Ciano, our daughter's husband. Mussolini found it hard to believe that he and the others (at any rate some of the others) could have acted entirely in bad faith, and he hoped that the preliminary investigations would reveal extenuating circumstances. When there was a lull in the violent controversy in the papers I preferred to say nothing, hoping and believing that a fair and sensible solution of the problem would be found. But events were fated to take their course, the Special Tribunal was set up, and one night my husband came home looking gloomier than I had ever seen him.

He told me that he had received Vecchini, President of the

Tribunal, of whom he had a high opinion. "If there is anything he can do without violating his conscience I am sure he will do it," Benito said. On the other hand the machinery had been set in motion, and the Fascists were insisting that those who had brought the régime to ruin after holding its highest offices should be brought to justice. Family considerations must not be allowed to stand in the way of retribution.

There was a brief interlude.

"12th December, 1943. Benito told us today that the danger of the occupation mark being introduced has been definitely averted; the lira will continue to be the sole currency in Republican Italy. 'An independent economy and its own currency are a free people's first rights,' he said. 'We have safe-guarded those rights.' He had previously told me of the many attempts made by certain circles in Germany to have the mark made legal currency, and I can understand that this success, for which we owe much to the Minister Pellegrini, is of political as well as economic importance.

"22nd December, 1943. I finished packing the parcels today. We have sent off hundreds destined to bring a little comfort to our people interned in Germany, soldiers whose families live in regions in enemy occupation and evacuees from the south. Christmas is close at hand and yet it is like spring here. What a contrast to the Christmas snows in my Romagna!

"26th December, 1943. There was a sad ending to Christmas Day. Mussolini was busy the whole morning at G.H.Q. After lunch the children called on cousin Vito who lives in the charming Villa Borghese on Garda Island. They drove off with Vittorio, and crossed from Punta S. Felice to the island in a motor launch. Vittorio, his wife and Anna Maria came back punctually at supper time. Romano, with a German second lieutenant, Dikaroff, Dr. Baldini and Orio Ruberti had preferred to cross the lake direct from the island to Gargnano. It was to be expected that they might be a bit late.

"My husband came back from G.H.Q. for supper and started playing with his grandchildren. We waited for Romano's party. On the lake there was no sign of the fishing boats with their lights reflected in the water. Time passed, it was getting late, and I was getting increasingly anxious, though I said nothing to Benito. Eventually I decided to have supper served. At table Benito immediately noticed that Romano was missing and I had to think up something to explain away his absence. Then I telephoned Vito, who confirmed that the four of them had left the island at seven o'clock in the motor launch. In the end we had to tell my husband the truth and we all began to think that some dreadful accident had happened. Benito nervously paced up and down between the windows. The staff, led by Vittorio organized a rescue party. We all gathered in the ground floor room while the hours dragged on like a protracted nightmare. My husband expressed his annoyance with Vittorio for having allowed his brother to be so imprudent as to cross the lake by night at this time of the year. Benito also authorized a naval detachment and a German photo-electric unit to join in the search. For several hours we were all worried to death until, about five o'clock in the morning, the door suddenly flew open and Romano, Ruberti, Dikaroff and Baldini, tired out and numb with cold, walked in. Benito, who up to then had been lavish with threats of punishment, simply clasped Romano in his arms, quite speechless. Then the truants told us of their adventure. In the darkness and fog they had failed to recognize Gargnano and gone past it. Then the petrol had given out and they had simply drifted along the rocky shore. A lucky change of wind carried them to land, but a long way from Gargnano. So they had had a long walk home."

CHAPTER XXX

THE TRIAL AT VERONA

WHEN OUR daughter Edda learned that her husband had been brought to Italy and imprisoned at Verona, while her children were detained at Schloss Hirschberg Castle, she demanded custody of them, being unaware that Vittorio had already brought them back. I was only too glad to have them at Gargnano until, a little later, I was able to take them to their mother, who was then under treatment in a clinic near Parma. Edda was allowed to visit her husband in Verona prison from time to time. The Germans employed a woman interpreter to keep watch on Galeazzo. Purporting to act as his secretary, she had a convenient excuse for frequent visits to his cell. On 18th December, 1943, Edda came to Gargnano to plead her husband's cause. The interview with her father was heated and most dramatic, but Benito, though realizing the dreadful family tragedy involved, explained as best he could, that it was no longer in his power "to distinguish between Ciano and the other accused, or to over-ride the legal authorities who were conducting the investigation". There were tears on both sides, but the drama had to be played out.

A few days later Edda, urged on by Galeazzo, devoted herself to getting possession of the famous diary, parts of which have since been published. The Germans knew of its existence and wanted to get hold of it, partly in view of their secret suspicions of the Duce. They intimated to her that they would favour lenient treatment of Galeazzo if she handed over the document.

Just as the Verona trial was opening, Himmler had Edda notified that nothing more could be done for her husband. On 7th January, when the trial was nearly over, she had her last meeting with Galeazzo. He gave her a letter enjoining her to flee to Switzerland and take the diaries with her. She acted on his advice and entered Swiss territory on 9th January, after a hair-raising dash across the border. In Switzerland she was interned and subsequently lodged in a nursing home.

Meanwhile, we at Gargnano were passing through tragic days, sadly awaiting the outcome of the trial. Mussolini had been given a document in Ciano's handwriting, and dated prior to 25th July, which proved his participation in the conspiracy which was uncovered in the session of the Grand Council. Benito afterwards handed it to me with the comment, "One day this will help to show what really happened and justify my attitude in Edda's eyes." During the night preceding the execution of the condemned men at Verona no request for a reprieve reached him. He was still at home, getting ready to go to G.H.Q., when he learnt that the firing squad had done its work. He wept tears of despair. We all wept.

"30th January, 1944. Yesterday I said good-bye to Anna Maria for a while. She had started some special treatment during her stay in Munich. The German doctors were very interested in her case and attended her most devotedly. When we had her brought back to Italy, it was agreed that she should return to Germany to continue the treatment. A few days ago Hitler wrote my husband a kind letter, reminding him of the arrangement. So Anna Maria has gone, sorry to leave us, but glad to resume the treatment.

"31st January, 1944. The Anglo–American landing at Anzio is the topic of conversation here. Benito does not believe that the enemy can march straight on to Rome. He said as much

the other day at G.H.Q. 'They could have exploited the surprise element, but they didn't dare,' he remarked this evening. I was called to the telephone a little later, as I was watching
a documentary film. It was Anna Maria, sending us her love
from Munich.

"5th February, 1944. At Anzio the battle for the bridge-
head is still going on. Mussolini is very annoyed with the usual
jitterers who are talking as if the Anglo–Americans were already
marching through the streets of Rome. But he is worried over
the food situation in the capital. He gets a daily report from the
Ministry of Agriculture and the Prices Committee, and discusses
them at home with us, but his main anxiety is over Rome,
where food convoys have great difficulty in getting through,
owing to enemy machine-gunning. 'The city must be supplied
somehow or other,' he said to me yesterday evening. 'If anybody gets killed in this job, he must be considered killed in
action.' "

On 1st March, the anniversary of the death of Gabriele
d'Annunzio, Benito paid a visit to the Vittoriale. Between the
Duce and the poet there had been unclouded friendship
throughout the period of the Fascist régime, despite the efforts
of partisans on both sides to disrupt it. On numerous occasions,
especially during the Abyssinian expedition, d'Annunzio had
sent messages to the Duce expressing his unreserved admiration
for him. The last meeting between them took place at Verona,
shortly before the poet's death, when d'Annunzio went to the
station to greet Mussolini on the latter's return from his success
at Munich.

"24th March, 1944. To the appalling domestic tragedy which
still haunts us, and at times seems more than flesh and blood can
endure, has been added the dramatic series of murderous fights
now going on not only between the Republican troops and
partisan units which have assembled here and there in the
mountains, but between sections and individuals in the cities.
These clashes are taking toll of Fascists, Blackshirts and officials
on one side and partisans on the other—all of them Italians.
We are heading for civil war. 'Why should the advocacy of a
political principle lead to murder?' Benito commented today.
The policy of the Social Republic and the Fascist Republican
Party is openly based on national reconciliation. That policy
has been enthusiastically welcomed; tens of thousands have
volunteered for active service and practically all the men called
up have duly reported. Unfortunately it was impossible to pro-

vide the necessary arms and equipment for recruits immediately after the upheaval of 8th September, 1943, because the depots were looted. But the general atmosphere is good, marred only by the activities of irreconcilable opponents who have stirred up partisans and agitators."

Ghisellini, the federal representative for Ferrara, was assassinated while the Congress was actually in session at Verona. Then Facchini, the representative for Bologna, was struck down. There were more victims, at short intervals, in various provinces: Resega, federal representative for Milan (whose death Benito felt very deeply), Professor Pericle Bucati, Manganiello the Prefect, Capelli, a journalist, General Parodi, Colonel Gobbi, Capanni, a representative, Marabini a Blackshirt officer. The heaviest blow of all was the loss of Giovanni Gentile, the world-famed philosopher.

"Yesterday," runs the entry in my diary under 24th March, "there was carnage in the Via Rasella in Rome. The reports rather vague. The victims are German soldiers. We always associate the Via Rasella with the gloomy period of my husband's illness, shortly after the Matteotti crime.

"25th March, 1944. My husband is furious over the Rome business. We had supper in silence but afterwards I got him to talk. 'It's terrible. They think they can treat Italians like Poles, forgetting they are only making new enemies!' He went on to explain, 'The German reprisals for the Via Rasella ambush have been terrible—they have shot more than three hundred hostages on the Via Appia. I was not in time to prevent it; all I could do was to protest. Why this outburst of hatred? The scoundrel who threw the bomb, killed about thirty German soldiers and provoked such a fearful reaction (out of which he has come scot-free), has not affected the course of the war the slightest, nor will the ruthless retaliation of the Germans prevent this sort of thing happening again.'

"27th March, 1944. I heard Vittorio hinting at the possibility of a fresh meeting with Hitler. Benito is reluctant to leave his post in these times, but there are many questions to be settled with Germany."

Mussolini did in fact visit the Fuehrer at the latter's G.H.Q. in February, and telephoned me from there to say that his talks with Hitler had been "very cordial". He seemed equally satisfied with the results but promised to tell me all about it on his return. He was away for a few days and came back tired out. The talks had been lengthy and binding commitments had been entered into, but he hated the cold, which always upsets him. Marshal Graziani had been present at the talks. Benito was pleased with the outcome: 'Not too much, but all that could possibly be expected after Badoglio's armistice, a source of unending trouble, now made much worse by his declaration of war on Germany.' "

I was particularly pleased to hear that interned Italian soldiers would be better treated in Germany. The fate of so many young men who were in no way responsible had been a major source of anxiety to my husband, and was a great obstacle in his path. One impending danger had been definitely averted: the industrial plants in the Po Vallé were not to be transferred, lock, stock and barrel, north of the Brenner. In the course of the talks, Mussolini had succeeded in persuading Hitler that "it was in Germany's own interest to have a zone of war industries dispersed over North Italy". The fact is that the threatened transfer, besides dealing a death blow to Italian economy present and future, would have also involved the transfer of hundreds of thousands of workmen, and Mussolini did not want to lose any more manpower.

The Duce and Graziani paid a visit to the S. Marco Division, which was training in Germany. In addition to its younger contingent it included a considerable number of older men who had been serving on the various fronts when the armistice overtook them, but had joined up again voluntarily in their eagerness to continue the struggle. Benito had found himself in an atmosphere of burning enthusiasm. A mob of officers and other ranks had chaired him and the spontaneous demonstration had moved him so deeply as to remind him of his popular triumphs in days gone by.

I find it difficult now to sort out my memories of the confusing events which followed each other with bewildering rapidity in that period of my life which began with 25th July, 1943, and was destined to end after 25th April, 1945.

One night a party of husbands and fathers from Bellaria and Cesenatico suddenly turned up at Gargnano. They had been travelling for three days, through snow and machine-gunning from the air, and said it was urgent that they should see the Duce. My husband was already in bed so I received them myself. I found myself facing a group of men in despair. The poor fellows had come to tell us that a German major had ordered the population on the shores of the Adriatic to evacuate forthwith the coast to a depth of eleven miles, as all buildings obstructing

artillery fire were to be demolished. "If you won't help us," they
pleaded, "we're ruined! We shall lose our houses, and where
can so many people find shelter in the mountains, with everything covered in snow?"

I was speechless looking into all those pale, drawn faces. The
next morning I arranged for them to see Benito, who took immediate action and had the order substantially revoked.

For some time I had not been well and was worn out by the
constant strain and all the ordeals through which I had passed.
I was also suffering from colitis, and had to look after myself.
I decided to visit the Romagna and try to recover my health
in the peaceful atmosphere of my native province. On 2nd May,
1944, accompanied only by my doctor, I reached the Rocca
delle Camminate. Spring was in all its glory.

CHAPTER XXXI

LAST MEETING WITH HITLER

TENSION RELAXED, particularly in Romagna, with the
approach of the summer season. There seemed to be a lull in
operations, and the front was apparently stabilized. Many of
those who had fled from their homes had returned and not a
few deserters had reported to their district depots. But life was
certainly no easy matter even for civilians.

Old friends from Forli often came to the Rocca to tell me
about the needs of the local population and complain of
incidents between the latter and German soldiers, usually provoked by arbitrary requisitioning of buildings, motor transport
and cattle. Naturally I could not turn a deaf ear to my friends'
requests. I remember the talk I had with a German colonel
the very day I arrived at the Rocca. Without mincing my
words I impressed on him that high-handed behaviour should
be avoided and the civil population allowed to carry on in
peace—to the benefit of the military operations themselves. The
situation was already difficult enough, what with the bombing
and machine-gunning from the air. Anything likely to lead to
friction should not be tolerated. I managed to get a stop put
to the searching of houses.

Benito used to telephone me daily and I made it my business

to see that I was in a position to give him satisfactory reports. But before long agriculture was faced with a new peril. The harvest prospects had been excellent, but it now looked as if the corn would not be gathered, or if gathered, could not be moved, as partisans were renewing their activities and threatening the farm hands with violence if they tried to get in the harvest. To make matters worse, fuel for the combine harvesters was scarce.

I succeeded in convincing the Germans that if petrol was needed for war, wheat was just as necessary for the people who had to carry on the war. This argument secured some fuel and I set an example by getting in the harvest at the Rocca delle Camminate, whereupon the farmers plucked up courage. To some of the most timorous I sent a few guards from the Rocca.

I returned to Gargnano, though not fully recovered, when the great Anglo–American offensive was in full swing. Rome had been captured and our foes were advancing towards the Gothic line. It was in face of these events that Benito had urged me to return. I found him very shaken by the loss of Rome. His furrowed brow betrayed his anxiety. "Rome is Italy and Italy is Rome," he used to say. "I tried to keep it supplied up to the very end. It was all I could do for my beloved people of Rome!"

He wanted to issue a clarion call to the nation to redouble its efforts. But even today, after the lapse of so many years, I feel that the loss of Rome was one of the cruellest blows he ever suffered.

There is no doubt that it had a most depressing effect. Much of the confidence which had been restored dissolved in a twinkling, and the phenomenon of partisan warfare reappeared in much graver form. Mussolini was shattered by the spectacle of Italians fighting each other. He spoke of the partisans as a father speaks of wayward children: "They'll realize their mistake some day."

It was he who insisted on the various deferments of calling-up notices. Many people criticized him for what they considered a sign of weakness, but he always answered that he was determined to pursue a policy of reconciliation. Even when men were tried for having arms in their possession or being involved in plots or ambushes, I have known him make every effort to prevent the death sentence when he heard of the case in time. "It is very seldom that we have the right to take human life," he would say. As far as I know he never rejected any appeal for a reprieve. Cardinal Schuster once submitted a particularly difficult case. Three women had been convicted by a military tribunal of mutilating the bodies of young soldiers. The crime was particularly horrible because of the ferocity and cynicism with which it had been committed. Benito took a long time to make up his mind, but ended by granting the reprieve.

One day he came home waving a copy of *Regime Fascista*, Roberto Farinacci's paper. There was a huge headline: "Duce's excessive kindness to Zaniboni." "Kindness can never be excessive!" he exclaimed, throwing the paper down on the table.

He was always very glad when he was able to tell me that some partisan group had returned to the Republican fold. He once told me that Hitler, during their talks, had remarked, "You are too kind, Duce; you will never be a dictator." Hitler once expressed to Mussolini an interesting opinion on Stalin. It seems to me that Hitler's opinion of Stalin, as given to my husband, is worth recording: "Stalin is the best of our enemies, both as politician and dictator." Benito himself had a high opinion of Stalin and his qualities as head of the Russian government, the Communist Party and the army. Neither for Stalin nor Churchill had he ever the harsh words he sometimes reserved for Roosevelt.

Foreign spies and Italians working for the other side often sent messages to the enemy by means of secret transmitters. Unfortunately, in their excessive zeal, some of their reports were inaccurate or utterly fantastic and resulted in the immediate bombing, usually indiscriminate, of places where troops or munitions were supposed to be concentrated. As often as not, the "targets" were merely houses, or even schools and hospitals. One example was the hospital of S. Dona di Piave which was hit by several bombs and almost destroyed. Two hundred patients, and the doctors and hospital staff lost their lives. At Gorla, near Milan, no fewer than three hundred little school children were slaughtered during another bombing.

About the middle of July 1944 there was talk of a meeting between my husband and Hitler. These trips to Germany were not much to Benito's liking, as he was always in the role of a suppliant pleading for supplies, arms, ammunition, fuel and relief for our internees. It was extremely distasteful to him. I was then worrying about his health. He had made a good recovery in the last few months, but I feared that the strain of another journey might cause a relapse. But he made it clear why another meeting was necessary. "There's too much defeatism about; I want to see for myself, instead of having to depend on diplomatic reports." In fact he wanted to know the truth about the much-advertised secret weapons, and see them with his own eyes. Our chance of victory was becoming increasingly dependent on them.

"20th July, 1944. A telephone call from Germany has frozen me to the marrow. Benito hinted at some serious occurrence but added that it seemed all over and I was not to worry. He would not tell me any more, and I am very anxious."

"24th July, 1944. Benito started telling me about the attempted assassination as soon as we were alone. 'It was sheer luck that we were not both murdered as the result of a conspiracy by some generals. Just think! Hitler was within a few feet of the bomb, and I wasn't there because an air raid warning had held me up for an hour at the Brenner. Now I understand why certain Germans hurried up my visit! Hitler came forward to meet me as usual, and I did not realize what had happened. I casually noticed that he held out his left hand and had his right against his chest. But he gave me such a welcome that we immediately started talking about something else. We met in one of the living-rooms at G.H.Q. Hitler inquired about my journey and then calmly went on to say that he had just had a slight accident, which temporarily prevented him from using his right hand. It was only then that I noticed how pale he was and pressed him for an explanation. He took me to the scene of the crime. The explosion must have been terrific, as the hut where he and the staff officers with him had been, was demolished. The assassins had certainly laid their plans well and were certain of success, because they had colleagues on every front.' 'But it means there must be traitors in Germany, too!' I exclaimed. 'You get treachery in all nations and at all times,' he replied. We changed the subject to the secret new weapons. 'They're there all right. I've seen them being got ready. I've even seen the "Death Factories" as they call them; I've examined plans and blueprints and watched experiments. The machine blows the world to bits and man has become the victim of his own progress. We are moving towards an apocalyptic phase of the war'."

My husband did not seem inclined to pursue the subject, and I refrained from indiscreet questions. But it cropped up again later on, because he was convinced that the secret weapons would be used at the right moment. But in fact Germany was not given time for a practical demonstration of that apocalyptic phase. What happened in April 1945 may remain a mystery for some time to come. Some have talked about the shortage of oil in Germany, but many of the new weapons did not need oil and were almost ready a month before the capitulation. It must be that destiny is stronger than man's will.

The agreement between Hitler and Mussolini came into force at this time, and resulted in about a million Italians previously regarded as prisoners of war being given the status of civilian workers. A source of even greater satisfaction to Mussolini was his visit to our army divisions which had completed their training and were about to return to Italy to go into the fighting line. They were the "S. Marco", "Monterosa", "Italia" and "Littorio". He was enthusiastically received by each of these units, and to each he made a speech of welcome and encouragement.

It was Mussolini's last meeting with Hitler.

CHAPTER XXXII

INTRIGUE

THE Duce moved to the Rocca delle Camminate at the beginning of August as he wanted to inspect the defensive line which had been thrown up astride the Apennines. He used to leave the Rocca every day for a tour of the forward areas.

On 7th August, the anniversary of Bruno's death, Mussolini visited his son's grave. This, too, was to be the last visit. In the next few days he spent the mornings on a tour from the Metauro river zone, across the mountains to the Muraglione zone above Castrocaro. In the afternoons he was usually alone, either in his study or walking in the grounds. He was seeing very little of his colleagues, civil or military, at that time and always rang me up in the evening. On his return journey to Gargnano he stopped at a villa in Emilia to meet Marshal Kesselring and Marshal Graziani.

"15th August, 1944. Benito is back at last; he came home yesterday. He has been telling me of many incidents during his five days at the front. Our men could hardly believe their eyes when he suddenly appeared in their midst. Over and over again there were spontaneous demonstrations of their affection for

him. The Germans, too, normally so unemotional, went wild
with excitement on seeing Mussolini and stiffened to attention
in the cramped space of the dug-outs. When the car was held
up he got out and walked, often finding himself where the firing
was hottest. 'It was just like the trenches in the last war,' he
said. On the Metauro front a whole battalion, ignoring the risk,
emerged from their trenches to give him a welcome. The
enemy soon realized what was happening and put up a fierce
barrage.

"20th August, 1944. Benito's return to Lake Garda has been
saddened by a tragic incident in Milan. The Germans have had
fifteen hostages executed in a public square to avenge the death
of some German soldiers killed by partisans. The news of this
fresh tragedy had been kept from my husband, so when he
heard about it, he was furious. He poured out his feelings to
me: 'The Germans have no sense of fairness at all. Why
humiliate a city like Milan with such an exhibition of summary
justice!'

"21st August, 1944. Mussolini is still raging over the Milan
murders. He told me this morning that he made a most vigorous
protest to the German Ambassador, Rahn, asking the latter to
inform Hitler that no one may carry out reprisals against
Italians on Italian territory without his consent."

As the days passed he became more thoughtful than ever.
I could tell by the way he talked from time to time that the
deadly struggle between Italians behind the lines was a constant
torment to him. Even at meals he sat gloomy and distraught.
He would sometimes listen to me in silence and then blurt out,
"What did you say?" I used to get very annoyed, but then he
would smile and ask me to begin all over again.

His temper was better at the beginning of the day, when
our grandchildren, always up with the lark, came down to say
good morning in their happy, carefree way and accompany
him to the gate of the Villa Feltrinelli. The doctor used to call
about eight o'clock, before Mussolini left for his office. But his
health was almost back to normal by now, especially after he
stopped drinking milk, which had been his main food for so
many years. A cup of tea was all he had in the morning. After
the doctor's visit, he generally took a short walk by himself
along the lake. From my window I often saw him, lost in
thought, in a garden chair by the clear waters. He would then
go to G.H.Q., come back for a frugal lunch, and return to
work. The evenings he spent reading, as at the Villa Torlonia.

Philosophy fascinated him and he regarded philosophical theories as mankind's highest achievement. Yet he admitted to me that he could not leave politics alone.

"5th September, 1944. Some Japanese submarine officers turned up at Gargnano today. They had left Yokohama over two months ago, and brought with them presents for the Duce from the Mikado—tea, oranges, cocoa and preserved fruits. Their very lengthy cruise through unknown waters strewn with perils of every kind is nothing short of an odyssey. Yet they describe it as if it were an every-day affair. The Duce gave them a warm welcome and invited them to the Villa Feltrinelli for the afternoon.

"I had rather a difficult job talking to them, though one of them had a smattering of Italian. He made a great point of telling me that the Mikado knew about my husband's special diet, and selected his gifts accordingly. About the cruise he said little or nothing, partly because, like all sailors, he was naturally reserved, but mainly, I think, from the reluctance of the Japanese to discuss military matters."

Enemy pressure against the "Gothic Line" increased at the end of the summer and culminated in a dangerous break-through, which brought them into the Romagna plateau and over the crest of the Bolognese Apennines. At one moment we feared that the Anglo–American offensive could not be held up and Bologna would be lost, laying the Po Valley open to invasion. Simultaneously the partisan guerrilla war flared up worse than ever, and clashes became more frequent.

It was sad news for us when we learnt that the Rocca delle Camminate, our best loved refuge, had been occupied by Polish troops. Forlì was lost shortly afterwards.

Fortunately German resistance stiffened and the enemy's advance was brought to a sudden halt just when it was looking irresistible. This new lull, which continued through the very hard winter, was received with general relief. It was at this time that a large number of Republican Fascists and army men began to press for a change of policy. It had departed from the principles laid down in the Verona Manifesto and there had been a return to the old rigidity and intolerance. Back to the ideals which inspired the creation of the Social Republic was the cry and there was a call for the removal of party and government leaders who were compromised by their records and no longer respected. Mussolini agreed and desired to make the necessary changes but found himself opposed by the conservative diehards and the Germans, inspired by the German General Wolff, a close friend and staunch supporter of Buffarini, the Minister of the Interior.

The previous Under-Secretary, Paolo Zerbino, and the present Under-Secretary, Giorgio Pini, had both fallen foul of Buffarini. As newspaper editors, both had campaigned vigorously in favour of adhesion to the Verona policy, even at the risk of being dismissed, as had happened to Mirko Giobbe, editor of *Nazione*, and Giuseppe Castelletti, editor of *Arena*, and was to happen to Concetto Pettinato, editor of *Stampa*.

My husband appointed a new Under-Secretary for the Interior as a start in the process of revising policy. But no one was more antagonistic to Buffarini than myself. I happened to know that, after having had himself arrested by the Rome Police Chief at the Villa Torlonia on 26th July, 1943, he had written to the Queen from Fort Boccea promising to keep secret certain documents which affected the royal family and Prince Umberto. At an interview I had with the Minister, in the presence of Prefect B——, at the end of 1944, I compelled him to show me those documents.

I personally held Buffarini responsible for being the leading figure in an intrigue centred round Clara Petacci, a young woman who, with her family, has been released by the Germans from Novara prison, where they had been incarcerated during the forty-five days of the Badoglio Government. The Germans —General Wolff in fact—had collected her belongings from Rome and taken her to Gardone where they kept watch over her, with one of their young officers acting as her escort. She lived in an apartment next to the residence of some Japanese attached to the Embassy. By a sheer coincidence, some relations of my daughter-in-law Orsola were living not far away, so it was not long before I knew of the reappearance of Signora Petacci.

After 25th July, 1943, when I first heard of the relations between my husband and this lady, I had been much embittered by the scandalous tittle-tattle in the press and very annoyed at the lies which then—and afterwards—masqueraded as the truth. At my first meeting with Benito at Munich we had talked the matter over quietly, and decided to regard the affair as closed. So it naturally came as a great shock when I learned from various sources, including also anonymous letters, that Signora Petacci had been seen in the vicinity of the lake. I did not know her exact whereabouts, however, until I found out quite casually during a visit to Orsola's relations. The very same day I spoke to Benito about the scandal which this situation was sure to create. He agreed with me and said that he had been to Gardone—where he had been taken by General Wolff—on one occasion only and then for the purpose of ending the affair once and for all. Buffarini promised me he would have the lady moved elsewhere; she could go to a castle in the Trentino which belonged to his family. Some months passed and I thought no more about it. Then I heard that, after a brief absence, she was back at Gardone. Sharp measures by the Chief of Police, Prefect Tamburini, brought him up against Buffarini and the Germans, and it was not long before he was dismissed.

Next I heard that Signora Petacci had had photostatic copies made of some of my husband's letters. I told him about it and he ordered his personal detective, Bigazzi, to see and caution her and get possession of the copies.

To be fair, she was less responsible personally than as a tool of shady political interests and financial rackets. Buffarini and his like sedulously cultivated her friendship and tried to impress her by posing as her protectors.

When Bigazzi reported that he had carried out his instructions, we were extremely grateful. But the reaction of the culprits involved in this tangled and murky business was not long in coming. Bigazzi was of course the first victim. Some pretext was found and he was dismissed. The same fate overtook Captain Hoppe, the German officer attached to G.H.Q.

One day I received a circumstantial report that a large motor launch had been acquired on the opposite side of the lake in connection with some hare-brained scheme to kidnap Mussolini. Exasperation over all these intrigues, on top of my acute anxiety as to the outcome of the military operations, made up my mind for me. I decided to see Buffarini and make him take me to the young woman. I have always felt that clearing the air is the best policy. Signora Petacci must have been shaken at the idea of my visit, as she kept us waiting some time. Then she appeared in a dressing-gown, looking wan and very disconcerted. She was accompanied by the young German escort officer, who was present during the conversation. I tried hard to keep my composure (the German officer had even searched me), though she fainted more than once during the long and uncomfortable interview. She certainly loved Mussolini (from her Novara prison she had written several forcible and courageous letters to Badoglio in his defence), and I tried to persuade

her that we must both sacrifice our personal feelings for the sake
of my husband's peace of mind and the good of the country;
otherwise we should find ourselves in peril and she herself might
get killed by someone. It was true that she was universally
hated, and some of our most loyal supporters had sworn to get
rid of her, to put an end to the scandal so unscrupulously and
wantonly fomented by backstairs elements to injure the Duce
and the Republic.

It became abundantly clear during the interview that the
girl knew Buffarini well, though the latter had assured me to
the contrary up to a few minutes before. She swore that her
action had been prompted solely by affection for Benito, and
that she had never received presents or any other material
benefits. She refused to believe that Mussolini too thought it
better to end the whole business, and insisted on ringing up the
Villa Orsolina. She got a chilling answer: "Yes, I know my
wife is there, but she is right. It has got to end."

It was getting dark when this painful meeting was over and
I returned to Gargnano and asked Captain Hoppe to see my
husband and tell him all about it. I was so distressed that I
had to take to my bedroom, and was soon downright ill. Benito,
after repeated inquiries from his office, came to see me himself.

He could not have been more concerned and showed his
affection in the most touching fashion. His words gradually
soothed my ruffled feelings though I could not help pouring
out all my woes. It was not so much the woman that worried
me as the danger, which I believed imminent, to my husband's
personal safety, having regard to that foul motor launch which
was supposed to be kept handy for kidnapping him. I told him
I could never stand another 25th July.

By now he had had enough of backstairs intrigues and
decided to remove the Minister for the Interior.

CHAPTER XXXIII

THE MILAN SPEECH

WHEN BUFFARINI got wind of the adverse turn of affairs, it
was to me of all people that he unburdened his woes. Placing
his revolver on the table he dramatically implored me to kill

him, swearing that everyone, his wife included, was against him. I was very annoyed, and turned him out. I continued to keep watch over Benito's personal safety, and had good reason to do so as I learned, just before he left for Milan, that an attempt on his life was being planned in that city. Fortunately, the plot was discovered in time.

To this day I find it hard to understand how I managed to carry on in such an atmosphere of conspiracy and intrigue. Certain Germans, under the inspiration of General Wolff and, to some extent, the German Embassy, were undoubtedly responsible for the fact that for some time now my husband had not been able to communicate directly with Hitler. At one moment he was compelled to send our son Vittorio to Germany to make sure that his letters really reached the Fuehrer. On another occasion he used someone in the Japanese Embassy.

Meanwhile I had to curb the impetuosity of many of our stoutest supporters who were furious at the state of affairs and thinking of kidnapping Signora Petacci, killing Buffarini and some of the Germans, and even staging a *coup d'état* with a view to removing such of the party bosses and the Duce's associates as were objectionable to the majority.

"16th December, 1944. Yesterday evening I argued against Benito's journey to Milan and got the reply: 'I've been shut up here too long; I must get in touch with the man in the street again,' a reply which does not exactly lessen my anxiety. I was worried nevertheless as my thoughts are always turning to what might happen in Milan. He was late in starting too—it must have been about eight—and the clear blue sky seemed a standing invitation to enemy machine-gunning.

"19th December, 1944. Had I not heard the frantic cheering of the Milan crowds on the radio these last few days I could scarcely have believed Benito's account of his experiences when he got back. It simply cannot be true that the whole country is against Fascism, or that everyone hates him. 'In twenty years of Fascism,' he said, 'I never had such a welcome. For some odd reason, General Montagna, the Chief of Police, had not been told of my visit to Milan till the day before. The proceedings at the Lirico were broadcast, so that all Italy suddenly knew of my presence. When I had finished speaking, the ovation was thrilling—an absolute triumph. As for the crowds, they were like a tidal wave. It was splendid to be back among the people, standing up in the car and hearing their shouts of loyalty.'

"He was a happy man as he told me of this and many other

incidents of the Milan visit. The crowd had taken him to its heart and it made him forget much bitterness. After the speech at the Lirico he visited a national restaurant, where he sampled the food which the authorities supply to the poorer classes at low prices.

"20th December, 1944. The Milan speech has revolutionized the atmosphere and even the most sceptical are recovering their confidence. Mussolini's statements about the secret weapons have satisfied people that they are not just wild talk, but based on solid facts which justify a hopeful outlook. He had mentioned the subject to me last July, on his return from Germany. When Vittorio and I questioned him about these weapons at table today, he replied, 'It's an amazing business but the enemy have asked for it and they'll get it! You'll see it all in good time.' He was not to be drawn further.

"The part of his speech which I particularly liked dealt with socialization. It takes me back to the old socialist battles I used to follow so ardently in our house at Forli, so many years ago. In those days no one outside Romagna politics had ever heard of us; Benito's life was one long perilous struggle, but how happy we were with youth on our side!"

Shortly afterwards, he received Field Marshal Kesselring at G.H.Q. In January 1945, Mussolini left for an inspection of the western sector, in the Garfagnana. After his welcome in Milan, he was keener than ever to get back to the common man and the private soldier. It was certainly not the best time of the year for a tour in the mountains; it was a very hard winter, and we had snow even on the shores of Lake Garda. I was left alone with my children and my thoughts.

After a few rather laconic talks on the telephone, Benito returned to Gargnano. He was pleased with the high morale of the troops in the line, but concerned over the situation of the civilian population in the Lucchesia, which was suffering from the bitter cold and the destruction of villages and devastation of the countryside by bombing and shelling. "Yet despite all this," he added, "the people are still loyal. Villagers shyly but confidently came out to meet me and some even kissed my hands."

He told me about a woman who had confided to him that her son, after serving for a time with the partisans, was hiding in the house for fear of being arrested. She begged that he should be allowed to join up in the republican army so as to put himself right. He immediately granted her request.

One day, just before the end of winter, he left Gargnano at seven o'clock in the morning to inspect a unit in training near Mantua. Shortly after passing through Desenzano, the little convoy was sighted by a fighter-bomber which swooped down to machine-gun them. Nobody spotted the danger until disaster was upon them. Prompted by my husband, his chauffeur swerved to the left, to get the shelter of a farmhouse. The plane fired at a car behind—General Wolff's—killing an officer and wounding a private. "My luck's still in!" Mussolini said when telling me of the incident as if it had been a trifle. He never mentioned it again.

What did infuriate him, however, was the events of 21st February, 1945, a day which has impressed itself on my memory. As I have already said, towards the end of the previous year, he had told the Minister for the Interior, Buffarini, that he no longer enjoyed his confidence. Buffarini, in the erroneous belief that time was on his side, had requested that his dismissal be deferred. But the situation could not go on indefinitely, as indignation with his intrigues and much too close association with the Germans had reached boiling-point.

On the morning of 21st February, the Duce accordingly sent him a letter of dismissal, which was taken by an official to the private secretariat to the villa where Buffarini was staying. Buffarini found various pretexts for keeping the official waiting, and the latter was left to cool his heels for several hours, while the Minister asked the German Embassy to intervene. The Ambassador, Rahn, did in fact call on my husband to plead the Minister's case. Failing in his attempt, he then asked that the announcement should be postponed for three days at least. Mussolini curtly refused, and gave an order for the news to be broadcast forthwith. He appointed Paolo Zerbino, then Commissioner Extraordinary for Piedmont, to the post of Minister for the Interior. But at the same moment he learned that Colonel Kappler, acting on orders from General Wolff, had arrested Tamburini, a former Chief of Police, and Apollonio, an official whom Buffarini hated. Angered at this interference, Mussolini, through Bonino, Under-Secretary for the Interior and Deputy-Secretary of the Party, protested to General Wolff and Ambassador Rahn.

Other changes in the government and the upper ranks of the Party were imminent when spring brought the resumption of the Anglo–American offensive and a rapid development of events.

"15th March, 1945. The military news continues to be negative. I do not need to read the newspapers, as a glance at my husband's face when he gets back from G.H.Q. is enough to show me that the situation is serious. The Italian front is on the move too.

"17th March, 1945. There is talk of our going somewhere else. The suite are particularly keen on the idea. What possible advantage there could be I do not know. Though the retreat continues in Germany and Italy, he keeps calm, and yet there seems to be one idea always uppermost in his mind. 'But why should we leave Gargnano?' I asked him today. He paused for a moment's reflection. 'It's an old project we're thinking of carrying out. Communications are easier from Milan.' But I realized that he himself could not make up his mind.

"24th March, 1945. A German officer who has taken Captain Hoppe's place at G.H.Q., called on Mussolini and then on me. He told me that the German High Command is opposed to the proposed transfer and kept reiterating: 'The Duce must not leave Gargnano.' It's my opinion too. I don't know why but I feel safer here.

"29th March, 1945. A party of women from the village has been to see me. Some of them had often had help from us, but others I had never seen before. They had heard rumours of the coming move and came to beg me to stay. They said that it is perfectly quiet in these parts, and the Duce was in no danger. Their sorrow was plain to see. I tried to reassure them, but their visit has upset me still more.

"1st April, 1945. An exciting Easter. After mass, I distributed gifts to the staff. Then came presents for our grandchildren, to the accompaniment of a cheerful din. Benito was glad they were here. We were still at table with the children when the sirens brought us back to the realities of war. The typical drone of low-flying aircraft followed almost immediately, Everyone made for the shelter except Benito, who took no notice of it. I stayed on for a time at his side watching the planes swooping low over the villa and then darting off to machine-gun cars on the road on the other side of the lake. They flew so low that we could see the pilots' faces. Columns of smoke rising from the distant shore showed where vehicles were burning. The machine-gunning went on all afternoon.

"5th April, 1945. Through the medium of Father P., a priest who shuttles back and forth across the frontier, we have succeeded in getting into touch with Edda, who has recovered in her Swiss nursing home. The move and the choice of new headquarters continue to be the subject of debate. There is a general feeling of helplessness which worries me greatly. The level-headed Benito tries to dominate the situation with his massive personality. But what lies ahead? The military position is crumbling, and even in Germany they seem to have lost all chance of regaining the initiative. I should like to tell my doubts and fears to my husband, but I realize that he shares them and I dare not worry him more.

"11th April, 1945. These spring days are filled with ominous forebodings. Life seems to have no meaning and the time passes under the shadow of the terror to come. So many people turn up for advice or news. I can only tell them we are all going, but I have no idea where. Our packing is a simple business as we have brought very little to Gargnano.

"15th April, 1945. Benito was really depressed today. He talked more about the future of Italy than of ourselves. 'Believe me, there's something in the Italian people that cannot perish and never will. Whatever they do, the Italians themselves cannot destroy it; it is a part of our history.'

"He told me he may be going ahead and we shall join him later. He also mentioned the possibility of a last stand in the Valtelline. I could not find it in me to argue with him."

CHAPTER XXXIV

LAST FAREWELL

"SEVENTEENTH APRIL, 1945. Mussolini left Gargnano today with a small escort. Though he assured me he would be back very soon, I was very frightened when I saw him off. He hinted vaguely at some important agreement he had to make in Milan, and mentioned the name of Cardinal Schuster. But today more than ever do I fear that he is being too honest when there is treachery elsewhere. He kept on repeating to me, right up to the end, that he would come back to fetch us.

"As he got in the car he seemed to hesitate, then came back, gazed at the garden and the villa and fixed his eyes on me, as if there were many things he wanted to say. Not a word passed between us."

Such is the last page of my diary.

I can still recall every detail of that crowded day. There was a vague sense of ill-ease in the house after he had gone; I was more worried than anybody else and could not make up my mind to start our preparations to leave. I was expecting him to come back from Milan, and still hoped that the decision to abandon Gargnano would be reversed. Never had the lake looked so beautiful as in those early spring days; yet nature's splendour sometimes makes our sufferings worse.

On top of all this, we learned that one of my nephews, a gallant soldier who had spent Easter with us, had been killed by partisans near Thiene. Beginning with the death of Bruno, our family paid heavy toll in this tragic struggle. We lost Germano and then his brother Sesto Moschi, an airman, who was killed in 1944. Tullio Mussolini, Benito's cousin, an air force major, was killed by machine-gun fire. Count Ricci-Grisolini, Edvige's son-in-law, was murdered. Later on, young Pino Mancini, Edvige's son, and Bondanini, a sixteen-year-old volunteer, were killed together with other comrades in the "Tagliamento" division.

On 23rd April I was in the garden when somebody hurriedly called me indoors. It was a telephone call from my husband in Milan. His voice was as clear as ever, but I could detect a tired note. "I'll be back at seven this evening," he said. I had all sorts of questions at the tip of my tongue, but all I could get out was the question whether we should be leaving with him straight away. "I don't know," he replied, with some hesitation, "I'll explain everything later."

Meanwhile his young private secretary, Gatti, turned up and started sorting out documents and deciding which were to be taken away and which destroyed. Barely an hour had passed before I was again called to the telephone. It was Benito telling me that he could not come to Gargnano because the enemy appeared to have occupied Mantua and Brescia was immediately threatened. I told him his information was wrong, but he insisted on our going to Monza. I informed Gatti. Meanwhile Prefect B., who had come from Milan to escort us, told us we must be ready by nine-thirty.

The sirens were going all the time, and we had to be careful to keep the windows closed while packing our suitcases and trunks. There were woebegone faces and tears all round us. Frightened though I was, I chattered indefatigably to all and sundry to keep up their spirits. The first to leave was little Marina with her mother and maternal grandparents. She hugged me tightly and sent kisses galore to her grandfather. There was much more she wanted to say, but they dragged her off, for time was running short. When she was some distance away, she started shouting, "Tell him . . ." but I could not catch the rest. Who knows what she wanted me to tell her grandfather. Then we all drove off; myself with Romano, Anna Maria, a Blackshirt soldier and Prefect B. went in one car, two Blackshirts and the luggage in another. The car lamps were not switched on because the alert was on. We were constantly passing large German lorries and troops going in the opposite direction. Enemy flares lit up the sky with their baleful glare before falling slowly—maddeningly slowly, earthwards. My thoughts were running on events in Milan. Why had Benito not come back to fetch us? Were the negotiations he had hinted at before he left holding him up? We were making for Monza. Gatti had told me we would be staying in the royal villa till my husband joined us.

We decided to leave the Strada Nazionale because it was jammed with military transport. We thought we should get along faster elsewhere, but no one knew the way and we could only try various roads. It was very late and there was not a soul about. We found the right direction at last and at daybreak we entered the park surrounding the royal villa. The guards showed us where we were to stop.

A man in uniform came running towards us; it was Baracu, Under-Secretary at the Presidency. "Where is the Duce?" was my first question.

"At Milan," he replied, adding: "We've been expecting you for a long time and were getting anxious. The Duce has rung repeatedly to inquire whether you had arrived."

We went up the villa stairs to two rooms set apart for us—one for me and Anna Maria, the other for Romano.

I was so tired and numbed by the journey and all the excitement that I dozed off for a few hours. Then I got up, my mind still full of doubts and fears, and went out into the garden. The kindly guards insisted on my inspecting the air-raid shelter, but I found it to be useless. I went for a walk, feeling utterly depressed by all this uncertainty, till I was called to the telephone about eight o'clock in the morning. It was Benito asking for news of us and obviously very concerned. He called up again at eleven to say he could not come to fetch us but would send Gatti to take us to Como. He rang up again at one o'clock.

Gatti arrived soon after. He looked grave, but was otherwise his energetic and confident self. Before he left I asked him if he would like to have something to eat. He had been on the move for two whole days, with no time for eating or sleeping. He said that he hoped to persuade the Duce to avail himself of a plane held ready to take off for Spain, where he would be looked after by his family (Gatti's wife, who was Spanish, was there). He also mentioned the negotiations in which Cardinal Schuster was the intermediary.

We left about six-thirty in the evening. The journey took over two hours and was not without incident. Eventually we reached a house, the Villa Montero, where we were told we were expected. But there were no signs of any preparations to receive us. Even lighting and bedding were lacking. Then Gatti left us. I was much moved as we parted.

"I expect some news very soon. Never abandon the Duce!" I said.

He looked me straight in the face: "I'll die with him, if necessary!"

And he was gone. A police officer had some things brought round from the Prefecture, so that we could get along somehow in that lonely villa.

All through 25th April we were alone. I had to buy a simple kitchen stove, as we had nothing to cook on. As we were told that there was no petrol in Como if we proposed to move on, I telephoned to the Prefecture at Milan and asked to speak to my husband. It was Vittorio who answered. He said that at that moment the Duce was at the archbishop's palace in conference with Cardinal Schuster.

That evening the news got round that Mussolini was in Como. He immediately sent me a score of loyal Blackshirts to act as our escort. I learned subsequently that he had rung me up several times, but without managing to get through. The Blackshirts brought us conflicting reports about the situation, but they included an alarming piece of news—a "Committee of Liberation" was functioning in Milan. Como was still quiet, as the German columns passing through did not stop.

When we retired to bed on the second night, some of the Blackshirts insisted on sleeping on the floor outside our door so that they could defend us in case of need. We were much touched by this proof of devotion. Yielding to the children's entreaties I lay down on my bed, but I knew I should not sleep a wink. I was utterly distraught. I still live through that night and the days following. Never shall I forget them.

My thoughts were with Benito going single-minded to his rendezvous with destiny, because he was determined to uphold the flag he called "the Flag of Honour". The children, in the happy ignorance of youth, were fast asleep. It must have been getting on for two in the morning when I heard footsteps and excited voices at the door. A Blackshirt tip-toed in: "There's a letter for you from the Duce," he said. I started to my feet, and snatched the envelope, recognizing Benito's handwriting and the blue and red pencil he had lately been using for his private correspondence. But I suddenly had my doubts.

"Who gave it you?" I asked.

"His Excellency Buffarini."

That seemed odd, and I questioned the bearer again. He said he was a police officer. I felt he was keeping something back from me. The name of Buffarini made me suspicious, as on the previous evening I had received a message from him urging me to follow him to the frontier by car so that we could cross into Switzerland together, and I had flatly refused. He was out of office and I was at a loss to understand why a letter from Benito should be sent through him. So I asked someone to remain with the police officer while I went to wake the children. We read the letter together devouring every word in our eagerness to get its full meaning. It ran:

"Dear Rachele, here I am at the last stage of my life, the last page of my book. We two may never meet again, and that is why I am writing and sending you this letter. I ask your forgiveness for all the harm I have unwittingly done you. But you know that you are the only woman I have ever really loved. I swear it before God, I swear it before our Bruno, in this supreme moment. You know that we must make for the Valtelline. Take the children with you and try to get to the Swiss frontier. There you can build up a new life. I do not think they will refuse to let you in, for I have always been helpful to them and you have had nothing to do with politics. Should they refuse, surrender to the Allies who may be more generous than the Italians. Take care of Anna and Romano, especially Anna who needs it so badly. You know how I love them. Bruno in heaven will help you. My dearest love to you and the children. Your Benito. Como, 27th April, 1945, Year XXII of the Fascist Era."

The body of the letter was written in blue, the signature in red.

I was stricken to the heart. The despondent tone of the letter, so unusual with my husband, made me feel that something terrible lay ahead and he knew it. I could not conceive that we should part like this, without a word between us, and did my utmost to get through to him on the telephone. While the pale and sleepy children read through their father's letter again, I kept my eyes riveted on the telephone while a Blackshirt was trying to obtain a connection. I was determined to speak to him and be at his side at this dreadful moment. Never before had life seemed so worthless and trivial—all I wanted was to share Benito's fate.

After half an hour's efforts we got through. Secretary Gatti was on the line.

"Is that you?" I asked. "To whom did you deliver the letter?"

"To a policeman."

"Then why did it come through Buffarini?"

I heard the receiver being snatched from the secretary and then quite suddenly Benito's voice: "Rachele, it's you at last!"

"But how did you send the letter?"

"By a policeman to be handed to you personally."

"It must have been taken off him, as it came through Buffarini; he's urging me to go to Switzerland with him."

Benito's angry reply was pretty forceful. He assured me that he knew nothing about it and that Buffarini did not come into it. He told me I was not to go with him, but adjured me to look after my own safety.

"But what about yours?" I retorted. "It's your safety that matters. It's you who are still needed."

He replied in quiet tones without a tremor that he was alone; even Cesarotti, the chauffeur, had fled. Then he added: "I follow my destiny, but you must take the children somewhere safe. I can only repeat what I said in the letter: forgive me for all the harm I have done you. Your life might have been quiet and happy without me! But I have always loved you— you know I have."

Then he asked me to fetch the officer in charge of the escort and adjured him to take the utmost care of us and keep with us till we are out of danger. I took up the receiver again, while the loyal, worried Blackshirts stood around. They soon grasped the situation and tears started to their eyes. I tried my hardest to convince Benito that all was not lost, as I had never heard him so apathetic:

12

"There are plenty left who are ready to fight for you and Italy; you have lots of loyal followers and the men around you will go to any length for you."

"I'm afraid they're all gone. I'm alone, Rachele, and I see that all is over," he replied. Then he asked to say good-bye to the children. Romano in desperation begged him not to leave us in the lurch. He told our son there was nothing to be afraid of; no harm had come to us even after 25th July.

I was appalled. No one left? But his personal bodyguard had been ordered to join him as early as the 21st! I had seen that splendid body at Gargnano, impatiently awaiting the order to leave. What foul intrigue had prevented it from keeping him from harm. No one left? Now I understand his despair. His world had crumbled around him. There is nothing more terrible than to realize that one is quite alone.

Benito had a few last affectionate words with Romano and Anna Maria, not forgetting some fatherly advice, and then bade me farewell once more: "You will start a new life. Hurry up! Good-bye, Rachele, good-bye!"

I remained by the telephone, utterly crushed, and heard the receiver at the other end being gently replaced, as if he wanted to break off the conversation as quietly as possible. The Blackshirts stood rooted to the ground and I looked at them in turn, but without seeing them. It did not seem possible that this could be the end and Benito should be facing the unknown alone, leaving us with an unpredictable future.

CHAPTER XXXV

TRAGEDY

THE SIGHT of the children brought me back to reality and got things moving again. I conquered the feeling of helplessness. I regained my self-control. I must do what Benito asked and save the children. And then I still hoped to be able to find him. It was three in the morning when we left the house to drive warily through deserted streets in what must have looked painfully like flight.

The Swiss frontier is very close to Como. There was no blackout in this neutral country and all the lights were on over the border. The region was swarming with the cars of the multitude seeking safety in the Swiss Confederation, lit up like a promised land.

We approached the Italian and German frontier posts and were received by some officials sent for the purpose by Benito. In a car quite close to us was Buffarini who suggested that we should join up with him to cross the frontier. I did not want to have anything to do with him, or even see him, but I had to intervene when my Blackshirts threatened to kill him.

We produced our documents but the reply of the Swiss police was short and sharp: "Absolutely impossible."

I recalled Benito's words: "They'll let you in. They've promised."

Everybody else was allowed through.

I felt vaguely relieved at the thought of not leaving Italy. It would be easier to get news of Benito. We turned back towards Como. The roads were packed with Germans and Italians fleeing in all directions. Several bodies of partisans were already streaming out of Switzerland and pouring down from the mountains. Stray shots could be heard, particularly on the outskirts, though Como itself was still quiet. We stopped at the Fascist Federation headquarters and went in. The place was full of people, either heatedly arguing what was the best thing to do or standing about. We were obviously wasting time so we came out again. Anna Maria sat down on the steps, and we too stood about, not knowing what to do.

The Duce had already left Como. This was obviously the lull before the storm. At dawn things livened up. One of our faithful Blackshirts insisted that it was dangerous to hang about in the streets. We held a conference and he advised us to take refuge in a house some way away, where he lived. We made for it. Our arrival caused something of an upheaval in the small, poorly furnished cottage. They had no food to spare, and I ended up by making breakfast for the lot with what was left of the provisions I had brought with me.

The Blackshirts went off to find out the news about the Duce and on their return said they had come to fetch us to join up with the column in which my husband was travelling. They also told me that our car had been stolen.

The sound of shooting came nearer. We looked down the road through the tiny window and witnessed scenes of panic. Our hosts were terrified and I spent all my time encouraging them. Helping others made my own anguish more bearable. A young boy, recognized to be a Fascist, was murdered before our eyes. A single denunciation was sufficient warrant for immediate execution. At intervals we listened to the radio broadcasting orders to hunt down the Fascists without mercy. From a nearby hospital badly wounded soldiers, clad in anything they could find, came flying out to scatter all over the town. The world seemed to have turned into a living hell. The children were panic-stricken.

About eleven o'clock our good Blackshirts came in to report that Pavolini has been wounded and could not get together the pre-arranged escort. At two they were back to say that it was impossible to join up with the Duce's column. So the unspeakable agony continued, hour after hour, day after day, night after night, and nothing but senseless fratricide. We lost count of time until that dreadful moment—I cannot say exactly when it was—when we were thunderstruck by the announcement of the murders at Dongo and Tremezzina.

"Justice has been done!" the voice proclaimed. I found myself thinking that Benito was now beyond the reach of human ingratitude and beastliness. He had given everything for Italy—even his life.

The men who died with him I had known for years, in fair days and foul, as his colleagues. Some were better than others and some I had liked more than others, but they all remained steadfast and loyal to the end despite the risk.

And that woman too, the woman whom they put alongside Benito at the very last moment so as to increase the scandal which she paid for with her life.

There is one thing which consoles me in my grief—Benito's favourite words: "Ideals triumph and endure beyond life itself when they are deeply felt."

I was prostrated by the news of the murders and barely noticed the shooting going on all round the house. Civil war was in full swing. My children never left me and their sobbing added to my grief, though I did my best to keep back my tears. The hours dragged on until it occurred to me that our presence in the house might involve our hosts in serious trouble. I talked it over with the children and we agreed that we had better put an end to all this uncertainty. So we sent someone to tell the Committee of Liberation at Como where we were.

Three men came and began searching the house. I kept as calm as I could to avoid frightening the children, but was under no illusions. While a police official was carefully going through the contents of my few suitcases, a young partisan relieved me of a miniature of Bruno, which I always carried about with me. He was obviously attracted by the frame, which looked like gold. "This belongs to the people," he bawled. "Everything belongs to the people," I replied, looking him steadily in the eyes, "because we have always given everything to the people and my son even gave his life."

The official intervened, made the partisan give me back the miniature and apologized. Then we were asked some questions and told to be available when wanted. The Bishop of Como, whom I had managed to contact, did not think he should assume the responsibility of taking in Romano and Anna Maria.

In the afternoon of 29th April we were taken off to the Como police station. No one harmed us, but we found ourselves witnessing some dreadful scenes. I was separated from my children and transferred to a small cell in the women's prison to which other women were constantly being brought. In the general upheaval nobody noticed my arrival. My fellow prisoners simply cast a glance in my direction and went on retailing the story of their arrest for the hundredth time. Only one of them looked at me in amazement and blurted out: "*You* here?" I tipped her off not to give me away and she moved off, sobbing quietly.

We could hear something of what was happening outside. Someone in the courtyard read out a list of names, and this was followed by a burst of machine-gun fire and, after an interval, the rumbling of cart wheels. The process was endlessly repeated and it went on like that all night. It was a ghastly business. The young woman who had recognized me was frantic about her husband. He was one of these in the courtyard, and every time the names were given out she clung to the window bars and screamed hysterically. Another woman was swearing she was a communist who had been imprisoned for infanticide and yelling to be let out. She was the personal maid of Luisa Ferida the actress. When the news reached us that both her mistress and the latter's husband, the actor, Osvaldo Valente, had been killed she burst into tears and protested that they had been kind and generous employers. Another fellow prisoner was a housekeeper whom a mere boy had denounced for having found a room for a Fascist a few months before. In all this tragic turmoil I kept comparatively calm, to the amazement of the others who kept asking me why I was not crying: "Haven't you left anyone behind?" The fact is there is a point where grief can do no more.

I passed another day listening to the firing and wondering when my turn would come to be summoned. Now that Benito could never return to me, I had lost all fear of death. I could only think of my children, taken God knows where.

It was the evening of 30th April. I was thinking of them as usual when, thanks to the good offices of a priest attached to the gaol, Romano and Anna Maria suddenly appeared. As I was getting them something to eat, with the help of a nun, a carabinieri sergeant came in and asked me very courteously to accompany him. This fresh separation from my children made me think my turn had come at last and I should never see them again.

We went down the steps and accompanied by two officials I got into a police car which moved off at once and eventually drew up at a fine villa in Como which I understood to be American headquarters. I was politely received by an Italian-speaking officer who took me into a room for what proved to be a long talk rather than interrogation. He was rather fidgety and seemed to me to be worrying mainly about the general situation. At one point he actually said, "How on earth did Mussolini manage to govern these people for twenty years?"

He told me not to fret about my children and later took me into the mess, where he gave me the place of honour and there was respectful sympathy on all sides as the tears rolled silently down my cheeks. I was thinking of Romano and Anna Maria. I was safe, but what about them? Somebody said in Italian, "You're not to worry; you eat." I managed to make them understand that I was wild with anxiety about my children, and they succeeded in convincing me that they were being taken care of too. I had plenty of smiles to cheer me up.

Half an hour later I was called into a little room which I no sooner entered than I found myself being hugged. It was Gina, my dear daughter-in-law and her parents, who amidst their tears poured out the muddled story of recent events. I heard the details of Benito's leaving Como (Gina was at the Prefecture when the incomprehensible order for an immediate move was given). "The Duce was very worried," she said, "because he was waiting for his own bodyguard which was coming from Milan. He gave me a smile when he saw me, and began talking. He asked my mother whether she remembered the card games they used to play at the Villa Feltrinelli. Then he advised me to leave Como. It was late at night and nobody had thought about bringing him something to eat, so I went myself into the Prefecture kitchen to get him some soup. Then they decided to move off at once, although the bodyguard had not arrived."

We sobbed in each other's arms just as when we shared our grief over Bruno's death. She kissed me again and again before leaving, as if she had a premonition that we should never meet again.

The next day Romano and Anna Maria were brought to me. They were both badly shaken, if not completely overcome by the tragedy. The Americans were most friendly and respectful. In fact they almost seemed apologetic. I did not ask what was to happen to us, or where we were going when, on the afternoon of 2nd May, they asked us to get into an Alfa Romeo. We left at half-past four and were set down about six o'clock at a building near the Castello Sforzesco in Milan.

At six o'clock on 3rd May we were taken in an open lorry for an all-night drive in bitter cold to Montecatini, which we reached at nine o'clock in the morning. There we were put up at the Hotel Impero. We were accompanied by a young officer of the Military Police, David Rosen, who was courtesy itself. We stayed one night at this hotel and next day were transferred to the Hotel Italo–Argentine where we remained till the morning of 10th May, when we were handed over to the British and left for Terni. After a non-stop journey, we reached our destination at sunset and were placed in the concentration camp set up in and around a synthetic rubber factory, the lay-out and equipment of which aroused their admiration.

We were given six rooms in the hospital, a small building overlooking the whole camp. From our windows we could see the crowd of internees, men and women, cooped up inside the wire. The news of our arrival soon spread to the inhabitants of that friendly little world and I received many touching messages of sympathy which moved me very deeply.

After a few days, I began to find idleness irksome, however; it is something unsuited to my temperament. I asked the Camp Commandant to give me a job. Surely help was needed in the kitchen, and I would welcome a chance to do something for the poor invalids in the hospital. After some demur, the Commandant agreed. The kitchen organization was at sixes and sevens; I set to work with some other women and we got things going as satisfactorily as possible.

Camp life kept me busy all day. At dawn, when I got up, I got a friendly welcome from the internees the moment I opened the kitchen windows. Work went on till late in the evening, and it was rather hard. There were six of us to provide for hundreds and, besides preparing the food, we had to keep the crockery and cutlery clean and see that water was taken round. With considerable effort, I managed to persuade the British commandant to make various improvements in the food and sanitary arrangements. I was often able to provide the traditional Romagna *tagliatelle*, much to the joy of our comrades in distress.

This hard and tiring work was a blessing in one way as it took my mind off my own private grief. It enabled me to think of others, and try to do some good. Nearly three months passed very quickly and I was sorry when we were suddenly told that we were going away for good, as I had grown very fond of the place.

When I said good-bye to the commandant, I made him promise that the conditions under which the internees, especially the young mothers and babies, lived should be further improved.

We were taken to Capo Miseno, on the Tyrrhenian sea, and went on board a motor launch which was waiting for us. The generous sympathy of the commander and crew, some of whom came from the Romagna, was most touching. Only at the end of our short sea trip did we learn that our new destination was Forio d'Ischia. I never liked islands and always hated the idea of being shut in by the sea, so much so that when my husband and children wanted to mock at this complex, they used to tell me I would end up on an island. Such are the whims of fate!

Ischia, dominated by the impressive Monte Epomeo, soon came into sight. It was the evening of 26th July, 1945. The tawny, sandy beach inside the little harbour was swarming with bathers. The commander of the launch tried to cheer me up, wished me luck and urged me to concentrate on the children's future. Yet even as the vessel approached the island and I began to take in its natural beauties, I knew my sorrows would ever be with me, whatever the attractions of this lovely and secluded spot.

During the summer of 1946, when Benito's body was reported to have been secretly stolen from Musocco cemetery at Milan and subsequently recovered, I recalled the closing words of my husband's book *The Life of Arnaldo*: "I have but one wish: to be buried next to my own people, in the cemetery of S. Cassiano. It would indeed be naïve of me to ask that I should be left in peace after death. There can be no peace for the tombs of leaders of those great transformations which are called revolutions. But what has been done can never be undone, whilst my spirit, freed of matter, after its little life on earth will live the immortal, universal life of God."

His wish has now been fulfilled.

INDEX